Barnes & Noble Critical Studies

General Editor: Michael Egan

E. E. Cummings:
A Remembrance of Miracles

Barnes & Noble Critical Studies published and in preparation:

Henry James: The Ibsen Years
The Silent Majority: A Study of the Working
Class in Post-war British Fiction
Wyndham Lewis: Fictions and Satires

The Fiction of Sex: Themes and Functions of Sex
Difference in the Twentieth-century Novel
George Gissing
The Historical Novel and Popular Politics in
Nineteenth-century England
Margaret Drabble: Puritanism and
Permissiveness
The Plays of D. H. Lawrence
Reaching into the Silence: A Study of Eight
Twentieth-century Visionaries

E. E. CUMMINGS:
A REMEMBRANCE
OF MIRACLES

Bethany K. Dumas

Assistant Professor of English,
Trinity University, San Antonio, Texas

BOOKS
10 East 53d St., New York 10022
(a division of Harper & Row Publishers, Inc.)

Barnes & Noble Books
Harper & Row, Publishers, Inc.
10 East 53rd Street
New York

ISBN 06-491822-X

FOR MARGARET

First published in the United States, 1974

© 1974 Vision Press, London

Printed and bound in Great Britain
MCMLXXIV
(See p. 14 for copyright acknowledgements)

B+T 2/15 4029

Miracles are to come. With you I leave a remembrance of miracles: they are by somebody who can love and who shall be continually reborn, a human being; somebody who said to those near him, when his fingers would not hold a brush, "tie it into my hand" –

E. E. CUMMINGS
"Introduction" to *Collected Poems* (1938)

Contents

Editorial Note

These *Critical Studies* will examine mainly nineteenth-century and contemporary imaginative writing, delimiting an area of literary inquiry between, on the one hand, the loose generalities of the "readers' guide" approach and, on the other, the excessively particular specialist study. Crisply written and with an emphasis on fresh insights, the series will gather its coherence and direction from a broad congruity of approach on the part of its contributors. Each volume, based on sound scholarship and research, but relatively free from cumbersome scholarly apparatus, will be of interest and value to all students of the period.

M.E.E.

Preface

Shortly after E. E. Cummings' death in September of 1962, John Ciardi filled a page of *The Saturday Review* with what was doubtless intended as a tribute to the memory of the man and poet. Early in the essay, however, he made this astounding statement: "Everything that need be said about cumming's work has been said by now." It bothered me then, and has worried me ever since. For one thing, Ciardi then went on to fill another two and one half columns with statements about Cummings. If, indeed, everything had already been said, he should have stopped four sentences into the essay. For another thing, the statement seemed gratuitously prejudiced against anyone who might come along later with a fresh insight into or a new fact about Cummings' works. Very recently, it has come in on me that the statement was also an extremely presumptuous one in connection with Cummings himself. To announce that a poet's future reputation must depend solely on what has been said about him within twenty-six days of his death is high-handed in the extreme. The possibility of posthumous publication alone makes the statement absurd on the face of it.

One does not want to make too much of this, of course; Ciardi made some interesting observations late in his essay, particularly in his closing paragraphs, where he commented on some of Cummings' poetic accomplishments:

> Because of his genius, e. e. cummings has written some of the poems in which our age will be remembered and made visible. And to the extent that every good artist's total work invents a character, cummings has created the figure of a kind of perception and of a kind of valorous honesty that will forever, by grace of singing

9

genius, raise readers in joy to a primary sense of their own lives. (*The Saturday Review*, September 29, 1962, p. 10)

However, I do want to call into question an unfortunate tendency —here found in Ciardi, elsewhere in others—to assume that because Cummings was not doing what other poets of the age were doing, he cannot be taken seriously. Ciardi, for instance, seems to suggest it is significant that "uncritical undergraduates" admire his work, while his poetry "tends to leave most of the faculty members shaking their heads." One wonders why Ciardi fails to mention "critical undergraduates" (there are such creatures) and whether he assumes some inherent superiority in critical judgement on the part of "faculty members." In my experience, faculty members who shake their heads over Cummings' poetry do so because they do not understand him—which is to say they have not read him—and because they consequently do not know "how to teach him."

Those twin deficiencies can be remedied by reading Cummings. One who understands what he means when he says "I'd rather learn from one bird how to sing/than teach ten thousand stars how not to dance" (II, 484—see Bibliographical Note) will be well on his way to knowing "how to teach" Cummings. Reading, of course, implies more than just looking at the words, and particular reading techniques are sometimes required for particular reading situations. This present volume represents an attempt to provide for the reader the necessary information for his development of the reading techniques which will give him the greatest insight into and joy from Cummings' written works, not just the poetry.

I have always felt very fortunate to have met the poems of E. E. Cummings at about the same time that I learned that a poem really is more than the sum total of its parts, that there is always a great deal more to it than *what* it says plus *how* it says it. A good poem is a living thing. Not everyone knows that.

This liveliness that is characteristic of all good poems is in an important way much more easily discernible in Cummings' poems than in those of some other writers, because of an element strongly present in his writings that is either simply not present in other writers or not present in anything like the extent to which it is present in Cummings. That is a strong sense of *play* as something intrinsically good, clearly positive. That was never the sole, or even the primary attraction of his poems and books for me, but it has always been an element strongly attractive to me. Play is kinetic; it is process; it is becoming.

Cummings' sense of play and his ability to express in language a sense of play in various stages of maturity have doubtless been partly responsible for his being treated as some sort of perpetual adolescent. Of course he was *not*, though he did have the very real virtue, as a poet, of being sufficiently interested in process and becoming that he could write poems in which the speaker is obviously exulting in a kind of adolescent awkwardness. The combination of that awkwardness with early sensuality can be quite appealing. In one such poem, which describes growing (up?) in highly sensual terms, the speaker describes his mind as being "a big hunk of irrevocable nothing which touch and/taste and smell and hearing and sight keep hitting and/chipping with sharp fatal tools." The speaker acquiesces in the process, concluding his description of what is happening to him with this statement: "Hereupon helpless i utter lilac shrieks and scarlet/bellowings" (I, 199).

It will be noted by the careful reader of Cummings that the thematic importance of a sense of play in his poems is that it is an *approach* to life and art, not just subject matter. In his approach Cummings never followed anyone else's rules, though he sometimes created stringent ones for himself. The result was that his "victories" seldom resembled anyone else's. For instance, he has been found "guilty" of lyric affirmation when more fashionable poets were writing poems of reflection or meditation. In many ways, Cummings was out of step with the poetic creeds of the twentieth century. Interestingly, though, he has always had a readership among the young; if I were guessing, I would say that that might make for a very long poetic life.

Cummings died more than ten years ago; in the decade since his death important studies have appeared and important materials have been made available, some that were not available when he was alive. I have learned from all the studies, and I have tried to take advantage of materials recently available. I regard this volume as a brief look at the man and writer E. E. Cummings as he was and grew and became. I do not think everything has now been said that needs to be said about him. I do hope this book may contribute to those statements which are surely to come.

BETHANY K. DUMAS

Fayetteville, Arkansas
January, 1973

Acknowledgements

It is a pleasure to thank the many persons who aided in the writing of this book. My particular thanks go to the persons who read the entire book in manuscript: Professors Margaret Bolsterli and Ben Kimpel of the University of Arkansas and Professor Norman Friedman of Queens College, City University of New York. I was encouraged and helped by Professors Carol Lindquist and James C. Cowan, also of the University of Arkansas. I am happy to acknowledge the help of Professor and Mrs Richard Wagner, who now own the house E. E. Cummings grew up in. They very kindly showed me over the interior of the house, and also the grounds; this gave me valuable background information not otherwise available. Valuable information not available elsewhere was also provided by Mr and Mrs Robert A. Cushman, also of Cambridge, Massachusetts, who also read and commented on parts of the manuscript. For their generosity in making books available to me, I thank the staff of the Southern University Library. Access to unpublished material was provided by the Humanities Research Center Library, The University of Texas at Austin. Copies of student publications were made available by the Harvard University Library and were ordered for me by the staff of the Hill Memorial Library of Louisiana State University. The staff of the University Library of the University of Arkansas in Fayetteville provided much assistance over the period of years in which material for this book was being collected. Both E. E. Cummings and Marion Morehouse Cummings answered questions and in other ways provided help. I should like to thank Mrs Verda Talton for her help in typing the early stages of the book. To my editor, Professor Michael Egan, I am grateful for help in making the final revisions. Others have helped—indirectly, if not directly—I think particularly of all the students whose questions prompted some of the answers in this book.

As the book was going to press additional information was provided by Professor and Mrs. Carlton C. Qualey (she is Cummings' sister) of St. Paul, Minnesota, and Miss Louisa Alger of

ACKNOWLEDGEMENTS

ACKNOWLEDGEMENTS

Cambridge, Mass. Mrs. Qualey read and commented on the first chapter. I am grateful for the help provided by all these persons; naturally, they are not to be held responsible for errors of fact or interpretation. Those are solely the author's.

For permission to use portions of unpublished manuscripts of Cummings, thanks are due to Alred Rice, Attorney for the Marion M. Cummings estate (quotations from Cummings' writings © 1974 by the estate of Marion M. Cummings), and the Humanities Research Center Library, The University of Texas at Austin.

For permission to use published material, gratitude is expressed to those persons whose works are acknowledged as follows: The poetry of E. E. Cummings is reprinted by permission of Harcourt Brace Jovanovich, Inc. and is from his volume *Complete Poems 1913–1962*, copyright © 1923, 1925, 1931, 1935, 1938, 1940, 1944, 1950, 1951, 1954, 1956, 1958, 1959 by E. E. Cummings; copyright, 1926, by Horace Liveright; copyright © 1963, 1966, 1968 by Marion Morehouse Cummings; copyright, 1972, by Nancy Andrews; and by permission of MacGibbon & Kee Ltd. (*Complete Poems*, Volumes I and II, 1968). Excerpts from the letters of E. E. Cummings are reprinted from *Selected Letters of E. E. Cummings* edited by F. W. Dupee and George Stade by permission of Harcourt Brace Jovanovich, Inc.; © 1969 by Marion Morehouse Cummings and by permission of André Deutsch Ltd. Materials from *i:six nonlectures* are quoted by permission of Harvard University Press, Cambridge, Mass., copyright, 1953, by. e. e. cummings. Materials from E. E. Cummings' *The Enormous Room*; *Him, Anthropos*, and *Santa Claus* (in *Three Plays and a Ballet*, ed. George J. Firmage, New York: October House, Inc., 1967); and "A Foreword to Krazy" (*A Miscellany Revised*, edited George J. Firmage) are quoted by permission of Nancy T. Andrewes and courtesy of Irving Fox. Other material from *E. E. Cummings: A Miscellany Revised* is quoted by permission of Alfred Rice. Permission to quote from *An Informal Memoir: The Best Times* (John Dos Passos, The New American Library, Inc., 1966, copyright by Elizabeth H. Dos Passos) has been given by Mrs. John Dos Passos. Material in Charles Norman's *E. E. Cummings: The Magic-Maker*, copyright © 1958, 1964, 1967, 1972 by Charles Norman, is used by permission of The Bobbs-Merrill Company, Inc. and Harold Matson.

14

1

Life and Times

From Cambridge, Massachusetts to New York City is no great distance, geographically speaking. The trip is five hours by train, one hour by plane. And so if we measure the miles from the academic enclave in Cambridge to Greenwich Village, we will find it no great wonder that a man might have moved himself from the one spot to the other in the course of a lifetime, even if that lifetime began back in the last century. But if we measure that distance metaphorically—not in time or miles, but in milestones—we must marvel to think that a man who grew up completely at one with his environment in the respected and respectable home of a professor and clergyman in Cambridge, Massachusetts—site of the oldest and probably most respected and respectable university in the United States—came to find himself totally at home in the very Bohemian and not at all respectable American equivalent of the Latin Quarter.

It is impossible to imagine E. E. Cummings having grown up anywhere except in Cambridge, and it is equally impossible to imagine his having ultimately lived anywhere else in America except the Greenwich Village area of New York City. His major works were produced there, and almost everyone now living who knew him thinks of him in terms of the three-story brick residence at 4 Patchin Place where for many years he and his wife Marion Morehouse lived in the ground floor apartment and top floor studio. To understand the importance of his pilgrimage from Boston to New York City (via Paris, where he was once proclaimed candidate for the mayoralty of what was once described as "the present literary capital of America"), it is necessary both to look at the events and episodes which preceded his residence in the latter city and to examine his later life in terms of his activities and his values, particularly, perhaps, as they occasionally differ from those of his parents and others of their generation.

Cummings was born October 14, 1894, at 104 Irving Street; as an adult, he was very proud of the fact that he had been born at home, rather than in a hospital. To him, the increasing dependence on hospitals and other institutions for the basic processes of birth and death signalled an unfortunate depersonalization in American life. He was, of course, fortunate in the family that formed the core of his own early environment. His father, Edward Cummings, taught at Harvard for a time (as an instructor, for a year each, in English, political economy, and sociology) and later was a Unitarian minister and an active student of social ethics. He became first a colleague of, then successor to the Reverend Edward Everett Hale, minister of the South Congregational Society, Unitarian, of Boston. Hale was a distinguished clergyman; he was also well known as the author of *The Man Without a Country*. Cummings' mother was the former Rebecca Haswell Clarke, of Roxbury, Massachusetts. He described her as a joyous, healthy, and generous human being—also a very courageous one. It was a large household. Cummings had one younger sister, Elizabeth; by the time she was born, the inhabitants of the house included her father, her mother, her brother, a grandmother, and one uncle. Later there were other family members, friends who came for long visits, and servants.

Cummings had many reasons to be proud of the fact that he was born in the family home. It was in many ways admirably suited for fostering the best in an individual. The house itself is of architectural interest. Built in 1893 in a type of architecture called Colonial Revival, it was an imposing three-story house of eighteen rooms, most of which contained fireplaces. Built on land which was originally part of the Charles Eliot Norton Estate, later known as the Shady Hill Community, the house was surrounded by other similar houses, each half-hidden by foliage and iron or wooden fences in a quiet street. The Cummings house was flanked by double pillars, and a verandah on one side faced a large oval garden ringed with a white-pine hedge and bounded on the outside by the three curving streets that come together there: Farrar,

16

Scott, and Irving. The houses on those streets stand today much as they did when first built, though some of them have been divided into two residences. The Cummings house originally opened onto both Irving and Scott streets. The Scott Street side has been partitioned off as a separate residence.

The community retains its original character; it has always been an academic enclave, dominated by Harvard professors and administrators. The first houses built on the estate were occupied by such people as the Nortons, the Eliots, and Francis James Child, of English and Scottish ballad fame. Later, William James lived there, as well as Josiah Royce and Frank Taussig.

The atmosphere in the household was generally progressive, the family being noted for its interest in the ever-increasing scientific knowledge of the day. There was a tool room on the third floor of the house, full of such interesting things as a pedal grindstone and an amateur darkroom. The first telephone in Cambridge was installed in the Cummings house. Ironically, these were things to which Cummings became increasingly hostile in his adult life. The journey from respectable Boston to Bohemian New York involved a number of attitude changes on the part of Cummings. In his later life, even as early as his college days, many of his attitudes and values were different from those of the family and community of his childhood. He was on principle opposed to the use of machines as substitutes for experience and as barriers against privacy. He once asked that Norman Friedman never read a work of his or look at a picture of his or, if possible, even think about him "while any mechanical unsubstitute for experience is anywhere even slightly audible" (*Selected Letters*, p. 175). And he was horrified to discover, sometime in the early sixties, that his postman had taken to carrying and listening to a portable radio as he made his rounds.

The nearby Taussig house provided athletic equipment for all the neighborhood children, all of whom were generally encouraged to enjoy and appreciate those things at their disposal. A diary kept by a neighborhood child in the year 1908 bears witness to the frequency with which all the neighborhood children spent their free time in the Cummings yard. They were allowed to run wild, digging up the lawn and turf without reproach, so long as they did not invade Mr Cummings' rose garden; he was very proud of

17

it and would come roaring out of the house if any of the children ran through it. There were many trees, even a tree house, in which "Estlin"—as he was known in his earliest years—was even allowed to spend the night alone, and in which he was allowed to have fires without supervision (when he was thirteen or fourteen) in the wood-burning stove it contained. The name "Estlin," by the way, was given him by his father in honor of Professor Estlin Carpenter of Oxford University whom the elder Cummings knew as a result of spending a year at Oxford when he was first holder of the Robert Treat Paine Fellowship for study abroad in the social sciences. Since Cummings' first name was Edward, his father's name, he was never called by it.

Cummings' father took a great interest in the household; he planned and designed parts of the house and actually built some of the furnishings and outside buildings. The tree house—complete with two doors, one at the ladder entrance, the other to the balcony overlooking Scott Street, and a shingled roof—was the result of his handiwork, as was the rather unusual garage, still in use today. Made of second-hand doors, it is roughly octagonal in shape, with a shingled roof. It was built to serve as the "auto house" for the Cummings' first automobile, an "Orient" acquired in 1907. He also did most of the building and repairing necessary to keep up the Joy Farm. There were a little frame house and a large barn on the farm when it was purchased. The elder Cummings put in windows, added extensions and another floor, and built two outside studies, one for himself and one for Estlin. Later he built a summer house on Silver Lake itself. Edward Cummings was so inventive and so skilled with his hands, that his abilities invite comparison with the better-known ones of his son. What the father did with his hands and with plastic materials, the son was later to do with his mind and words.

There were pets—two dogs, a cat, goldfish, and rabbits, kept in a pen under the house in the back yard. And there were books, of course, the books which formed Cummings' earliest taste in reading. As an adult, Cummings expressed gratitude for those first literary experiences. He was, he said, particularly grateful that he had grown up protected from what he liked to call "the uncomic nonbooks." He pointed out in a lecture at Harvard in 1952 that his imagination had probably benefitted from being spared the paltry supermen, shadowy space-cadets, trifling hyperjunglequeens, and pantless pantherwomen characteristic of such publications. Instead he read, and had read to him at an early age, myths and animal stories and writers like Scott, Dickens, Defoe, Swift, and Verne. He singled out for mention also *The Pickwick Papers, Robinson Crusoe, The Swiss Family Robinson, Twenty Thousand Leagues Under the Sea, The Holy Bible, and The Arabian Nights.* And he says he read much poetry. In general, it can be said that he read what was standard for members of his class and of his time.

Another form of literature by which he was probably indirectly influenced was the versification which accompanies many children's games. It sometimes occurs as a counting rhyme; in other games, it may be a challenge or an announcement. For instance, the children of his neighborhood played a tag game in the winter called "Hill Dill." The person who was "it" issued a challenge in this form:

> Hill dill,
> Come over my hill,
> Or else I'll catch you standing still!

And the children of nearby Somerville used to parade on May Day, chanting rhymes as they marched along in colored tissue paper crowns, wands with streamers etc.:

> Who are we?
> Who are we?
> We are Somerville,
> Don't you see?
>
> Are we in it?
> Well I guess we are.
> Somerville, Somerville,
> Rah! Rah! Rah!

Finally, there were family friends and associates, some of whom had a direct influence on Cummings' development as a poet, and all of whom probably had an indirect influence on his general intellectual and emotional development. William James had introduced Cummings' mother and father; Edward Everett Hale has been mentioned; Charles Eliot Norton, in whose woods Cummings used to play, lived nearby; Professor Royce introduced Cummings simultaneously to Dante Gabriel Rossetti and the sonnet.

19

Cummings later said that he never made a conscious decision to be a poet. He remembered that he always wrote poetry, and he also said that as far back as he could remember he was writing and painting. He even traced three poetic periods in his early life, the first two of which he described in detail. The first was from his very young years and was quite individualistic; two couplets preserved by his mother testify to early fearless expression and keen observation. In the first (and earlier) of them there is a suggestion of what was to become characteristic Cummings movement:

> O, the pretty birdie,O;
> with his little toe,toe,toe!
> (i:six nonlectures, p. 28)

The second may be read as a striving for the wit that was to be characteristic of other later poems:

> there was a little farder
> and he made his mudder harder
> (i:six nonlectures, p. 28)

The credo of the second poetic period dictated that the only thing which mattered about a poem was its literal meaning. An example of a "good" poem was one which did good. Therefore, a poem like Julia Ward Howe's "Battle Hymn of the Republic" was to be preferred to poems which had no practical good as their ends. During this period, the young Cummings composed "canticles of comfort" for the benefit of persons whose relatives had recently died, implored healthy Christians to aid poor whites suffering from hookworm (which he pompously designated the Curse of the Worm), and took every opportunity to urge "right-minded patriots" to abstain from the use of fireworks on July 4. He later suggested, more seriously than not, that he had—by the age of six or seven—reached the precise stage of "intellectual development" beyond which Marxist adults are supposed not to go.

Fortunately there was soon a third period, initiated when Cummings was presented with a copy of "The Rhymster." At that point, he said, his energies were for the first time directed from *what* to *how*, from *substance* to *structure*. He learned early in this period that there are many poetic forms, and that each form has an existence beyond the use to which it is or is not put. It was in this

20

period that the encounter with Professor Royce occurred. Royce, having learned that "Estlin" wrote poetry, inquired whether he were familiar with Rossetti's sonnets. Cummings was not. The two repaired to Professor Royce's study, where he read a number of the sonnets aloud. Cummings later suggested that that early experience was responsible for the large number of sonnets he had written during his lifetime.

The young Cummings' early years were happy ones, partly because his creative energies were stimulated and encouraged by almost everyone with whom he came in contact. It is particularly interesting to note that though he came to rebel against many of the traditional values and virtues of his childhood—the Puritan work ethic, notably—he was never sorry that as a child he had been able to depend upon the persons and things he had been able to depend upon the persons and things in his immediate environment. He always had a strong sense of home, which he equated with privacy. At the conclusion of a successful battle with the city of New York later in his life, Cummings wrote a letter thanking the mayor, Robert Wagner, for his help in saving Patchin Place from "renovation." In it, he stated his conviction that nothing is so important to a human being as privacy, since without privacy it is impossible for individuals to exist (*Selected Letters*, p. 274).

Cummings' formal schooling began at a private school in Cambridge. There he claimed to have learned nothing; all he later remembered were tears and nosebleeds. After that came several public schools, at one of which, the seven-grade Agassiz School, Cummings encountered Miss Maria Baldwin, the Negro principal remembered for her understanding nature, her teaching ability, and her administrative talents. Later, in one of the grades of the Peabody School, he was taught by an equally remarkable teacher still remembered for her ability to teach, year after year, a list of poems with exactly the same inflection. They are still recited at dinner parties in Cambridge. The list included works by Shakespeare (an extract from *Julius Caesar*), Emerson ("The Rhodora"), Holmes ("Old Ironsides" and "The Chambered Nautilus"), Longfellow ("Evangeline"), Lincoln ("The Gettysburg Address"), Gray (extract from "Elegy: Written in a Country Churchyard"), and Bryant (extract from "Thanatopsis"). Finally, there was the Cam-

21

bridge High and Latin School, where the most important thing Cummings learned was Greek. He was being prepared for Harvard, of course; it was inevitable that he go there, and even as a baby he had worn a white sweater on which his mother had embroidered a red H.

He entered Harvard in the Fall of 1911 and was quite happy there, making new friends, meeting new books, and appearing in the rival student publications, *The Harvard Advocate* and the short-lived *Harvard Monthly*. His first published poems appeared in those periodicals; they show quite plainly the various literary influences working on him. Those early published poems are characterized by ballad subjects and archaic language. There are exercises of various sorts, one in the Spenserian stanza. The poems are not, on the whole, particularly good; they are important primarily because they indicate that Cummings was writing a great deal and was experimenting with many stanza forms. He was also studying enough to graduate *magna cum laude* in 1915.

Through his association with the two student magazines, Cummings met fellow writers, some of whom were to be important later as both writers and editors. The editors of the *Monthly*—such men as Gilbert Seldes, Robert Nathan, John Dos Passos, and Robert Hillyer—tended to feel that editors of the "other magazine," the *Advocate*, were clubmen and athletes, followers of Teddy Roosevelt who were not truly dedicated to the art of letters. Perhaps that set of opinions was justified; at any rate, the *Monthly* did count among its contributors more writers and editors, one of whom, Sibley Watson, later joined with Scofield Thayer to transform *The Dial* into an excellent and important literary journal. The editors of the *Advocate*, on the other hand, felt that the staff of the *Monthly* were devotees of art for art's sake and that they were probably aesthetes and pacifists, at best. The *Advocate* ultimately made the bigger appeal to undergraduates; Cummings had five works published in it, including his commencement address on "The New Art." In retrospect, it seems well that the two publications never followed the suggestion made by the daily *Crimson* that they merge. They served similar purposes, and the resulting rivalry seems to have been a healthy stimulus to creation.

Other associations were important and interesting. For instance, there is Cummings' remembrance of his first encounter with T. S.

Eliot. He was a member of the Cambridge Dramatic Club and in 1913 he played the role of Ernest, a footman, in a production of Jerome K. Jerome's *Fanny and the Servant Problem.* He said later that he remembered two things about the production: one was that he was kissed by the very beautiful leading lady, the other was that the hero—whom he remembered only as Lord Somebody or other—was brilliantly played by a cold and somewhat aloof person: Thomas Stearns Eliot. The two did not meet formally for several decades.

It is interesting to reconstruct the mood of those pre-World War I days at Harvard. The "dandies," as Malcolm Cowley has called these young poets in the New England tradition, were never a homogeneous group. Cummings early seemed not to be quite of his own generation. John Dos Passos recently recalled some ways in which Cummings' interests were different from those of his contemporaries. In *An Informal Memoir: The Best Times* (1966), he says that everyone else lived in the eighteen-nineties as much as possible, preferring to read *The Yellow Book, The Hound of Heaven,* and Machen's *Hill of Dreams,* all of which seemed more important than news of the massacres around Verdun. Cummings lived deep in Greek and in his developing interest in his special poetic typography.

All this was important; equally important to Cummings was his first taste of independence, achieved in his senior year when he moved from home to a room in the Yard, on the second floor of Thayer Hall. Though his home life had not been severely restricted, he had grown up as the son of a minister, and he doubtless felt freer to come and go as he pleased after his move. He began to explore aspects of Boston that he had not known before; these included the pleasures of eating and drinking in German, Chinese, and Greek restaurants, and the joys of burlesque as they were presented in the Howard Athenaeum at Scollay Square, the "Old Howard" of several of Cummings' poems. They also included partying on a scale seldom possible in a parental home and such incidents as that described by Malcolm Cowley: "One night the Boston police were embarrassed to find his father's car, with its clergyman's license plates, parked outside a joint near Scollay Square. Cummings and Dos Passos, both virgins at the time, were not 'upstairs'; they were drinking in the parlor while holding a polite conversation with the madam." ("Cummings: One Man Alone," *The Yale Review*, LXII, No. 3 [March 1973], p. 334.)

Two kinds of houses figured prominently in Cummings' young adult life and in his early poetry. His attraction to the one kind requires no explanation. His attraction to the second kind calls for some comment, however. The importance of burlesque to Cummings has never received the attention it should. The omission is strange, because as early as 1946 its importance was pointed out by critics Horace Gregory and Marya Zaturenska. And Cummings himself frequently spoke of his "respect" for burlesque as an art form. Gregory and Zaturenska suggested in an article in the Cummings number of *The Harvard Wake* (No. 5, Spring, 1946) that many of his poems appear to have been written

> in the same spirit that graced the songs and speeches of the *commedia dell' arte*, which travelled up from Italy in the sixteenth century to entertain the peoples of the rest of Europe. And it has been said that the *commedia dell' arte* (and in this respect its relationship to Cummings' poetry is pertinent) was an ancestor of the American stock-company burlesque show. The characters who speak or are referred to in Cummings' verse might well have been reciting the traditional roles that the *commedia dell' arte* provided four centuries ago; and the devices that the verses themselves employ, the almost manual skill of transposed words, phrases, and of rhymes, have the same quality that we enjoy when we witness a performance of Charles Chaplin in his early films or one given by Robert Edward (Bobby) Clark in a musical revue. And Cummings has always been careful never to permit the central figure of his young lover to slip into the unwitting fatuousness of middle age. ("E. E. Cummings, American Poet of the Commedia Dell' Arte," p. 72. This later appeared in *A History of American Poetry: 1900–1940*.)

By the end of 1915, Cummings was beginning to be heavily influenced by what he was learning of modern music and poetry and painting. Through S. Foster Damon he became familiar with *Ripostes*, by Ezra Pound, and ultimately with the Imagist credo, issued by Pound and his associates in England. Through Theodore Miller he became familiar with the poems of Catullus, Horace, and Sappho in the original Latin and Greek, and also John Keats, from whom he learned so much, as we shall see. The echoes from

24

the poetry of John Milton which occur at this time suggest that he was also an important influence.

When Cummings graduated, in English and the classics, he was invited to speak at the Commencement celebration. His address, "The New Art," displays a rather extraordinary perception. It was also at the time rather high in shock value. Before reading two poems by Amy Lowell, whose brother was present as President of Harvard, he made the statement that Amy Lowell's "Grotesque" showed development from the normal to the abnormal. His reading of the poem, which begins with the line "Why do the lilies goggle their tongues at me," stunned the audience. Professor Damon, the biographer of Amy Lowell, reports that

> One aged lady . . . was heard to remark aloud: "Is that our president's sister's poetry he is reading? . . . Well, *I* think it is an *insult* to our president!" Meanwhile, the president's face, on which all eyes were fixed, was absolutely imperturbed. But one of the Boston newspapers, which did not truckle to the Brahmins, came out with the headlines recalled as "Harvard Orator Calls President Lowell's Sister Abnormal!" (*Amy Lowell*, p. 312)

The point being made by Cummings was that the poet had achieved the effect she had by employing grotesque images in order to move beyond the conventional. He also read "The Letter," suggesting that its particular success would not have been possible in any other period:

> This poem is superb of its kind. I know of no image in all realistic writing which can approach the absolute vividness of the first two lines. The metaphor of the chafed heart is worthy of any poet; but its fanciful development would have been impossible in any literature except this ultramodern. (*A Miscellany Revised*, p. 9)

He then read from two other authors, Donald Evans and Gertrude Stein, suggesting that the former had written poems in which there were literary parallels to the "sound painters," while the works of the latter were the result of carrying the logic of literary sound painting to its extreme. Convinced that the results were indeed logical, he was not prepared to admit that they were art. After quoting from "Tender Buttons," he concluded his discussion of literature thus:

25

The book from which these selections are drawn is unquestionably a proof of great imagination on the part of the authoress, as anyone who tries to imitate her work will discover for himself. Here we see traces of realism, similar to those which made the "Nude Descending a Staircase" so baffling. As far as these "Tender Buttons" are concerned, the sum and substance of criticism is impossible. The unparalleled familiarity of the medium precludes its use for the purpose of aesthetic effect. And here, in their logical conclusion, impressionistic tendencies are reduced to absurdity. (*A Miscellany Revised*, p. 10)

Cummings' discussion of "The New Art" included comments on painting, sculpture, architecture, the stage, literature, and music. In addition to the literary figures whose work he discussed, he also discussed works by Cézanne, Matisse, Brancusi, César Franck, Erik Satie, Schönberg, Marcel Duchamp, and Stravinsky. He concluded with some general remarks on the future of art:

The question now arises: how much of all this is really Art?
The answer is: We do not know. The great men of the future will undoubtedly profit by the experimentation of the present period, for this very experimentation is the logical unfolding of sound tendencies. That the conclusion is in a particular case absurdity does not in any way vitiate the value of the experiment providing we are dealing with sincere effort. The New Art, discredited though it be by fakirs and fanatics, will appear in its essential spirit to the unprejudiced critic as a courageous and genuine exploration of untrodden ways. (*A Miscellany Revised*, pp. 10–11)

The year was 1915; Cummings was twenty years old. It was a rather extraordinary performance. As Cummings' biographer Charles Norman has said,

It is a remarkable picture—the straight youthful figure with the erect blond head telling the Cambridge ladies—and gentlemen—who had gotten as far as John Singer Sargent, perhaps, but who undoubtedly knew Longfellow, what the new art was. Cummings' reading and discussions, his attendance at concerts and exhibitions, had borne strange and exhilarating fruit. (*E. E. CUMMINGS: The Magic-Maker*, p. 46)

Cummings stayed on at Harvard for one more year, during which he earned an M.A. degree from the Graduate School of

Arts and Sciences and helped to organize the Harvard Poetry Society. Appropriately, one of Cummings' first really fine poems appeared in *The Harvard Monthly* for March, 1916—"All in green went my love riding." It eventually appeared in his first full volume of poetry, *Tulips and Chimneys* (1923).

Eight Harvard Poets was apparently conceived during Cummings' last year at Harvard. Stewart Mitchell first had the idea of collecting into a book the poems of some of those who had been associated at Harvard. Cummings had eight poems in the book, four of them sonnets which rank with the best of his early poems. Of the eight poems which appeared in *Eight Harvard Poets*, seven were later collected. Since they are discussed in the next chapter, it will be sufficient here to note that the publication of *Eight Harvard Poets* quite clearly marks the end of Cummings' student days. The books which follow are those of a poet and writer. (The book, incidentally, bore other fruit; there was later an *Eight More Harvard Poets*; it included poems by Malcolm Cowley and John Brooks Wheelwright, among others.)

In 1917 Cummings went to New York City for the first time, and its effect was staggering. "In New York I also breathed: and as if for the first time," he later said (*i:six nonlectures*, p. 52). He bore with him letters of introduction from various literary figures. Letters from Amy Lowell which preceded him give evidence that she, at least, did not resent his earlier comments about her poetry; she recommended Cummings to the attention of three magazine editors, the editors of *Century*, *Scribner's Magazine*, and *Craftsman*, to each of whom she sent the following letter:

> I am taking the liberty of giving a letter of introduction to you to a young Harvard graduate, named Erstline [*sic*] Cummings. He has been specializing in English, I believe, and had one of the Commencement parts last year, in which I hear he was very brilliant. He is extremely interested in all forms of the New Poetry, but I do not think confines himself to that branch of literature. He is very anxious to get something to do on a magazine, and although I have very little hope that you will have anything to give him, perhaps you would be so kind as to see him for a few minutes and give him some excellent advice. At any rate, I hope that I am not trespassing upon a very slight acquaintance; if I am, pray ignore both this note and the letter he will bring you. (*Amy Lowell*, p. 363)

He did work briefly at the firm of P. F. Collier & Son, Inc., which did mail order business in books. After three months, however, he decided his position was unnecessary and "fired" himself. It was the first and last regular job he had.

At that time it was becoming increasingly clear that the United States was shortly due for a more active part in the war. Enthusiasm for army service was not high among young writers in America, yet there was a strong desire to be on the scene. As a result, some of them joined other services, while others enlisted in the American Field Service or in an ambulance corps. William Faulkner, for instance, slipped into Canada and joined the Canadian Air Force; Malcolm Cowley enlisted in the French military transport. Cummings was one of many who enlisted in the Norton Harjes Ambulance Corps. He later said that he did so in order to avoid the U.S. Army. John W. Aldridge has since analyzed the motivation of Cummings and others who went into the Corps:

> It was no accident that so many of these young men chose to volunteer with the Norton Harjes. . . . They were still tentative, uncertain about the war and their place in it. They wanted romance without danger. As American gentlemen volunteers they got what they wanted. They were onlookers . . . this led to their having what Malcolm Cowley called the "spectatorial attitude" (*Exile's Return*). (*After the Lost Generation*, pp. 4–5)

Cummings may have begun as a detached onlooker, but he very soon found himself directly involved in the business of a nation at war. He spent several months in a French concentration camp; after his release he returned to the United States and eventually ended up in the U.S. Army, anyway. The extraordinary events, which led to his next book, began when Cummings sailed for France in April, 1917. On *La Tourraine* Cummings met William Slater Brown, with whom and largely because of whom he was eventually to be arrested by French police on suspicion of treason. Cummings told the entire story of his arrest and imprisonment in *The Enormous Room*. His father told the story of his struggle to get Cummings released from the prison at *La Ferté Macé* in a 1922 Foreword to the book. Charles Norman's biography documents much of the correspondence that took place before Cummings was released.

What apparently happened was that indiscretions on the part of Brown and misunderstandings on the part of the French authorities led to Cummings' totally unjust imprisonment. Both Cummings and Brown were unhappy with their work as members of the Norton Harjes ambulance corps, largely because their section chief regarded it as his duty to keep them away from "those dirty Frenchmen" with whom they were working and for whose benefit they had presumably volunteered, while they, on the other hand, seized "every opportunity for fraternization." His dissatisfaction had prompted Brown to write some rather indiscreet letters to friends back in America. His initial indiscretion was compounded by his choice of friends: one of them was Emma Goldman, internationally known revolutionary. The letters had, inevitably, been seized by over-jealous French censors, and Brown was arrested on suspicion of treason. Cummings' arrest resulted from the application of the principle of guilt by association. His dissatisfaction with his work may be gauged by his comment early in *The Enormous Room* that the arrest amounted to his "being yanked from the putrescent banalities of an official non-existence into a high and clear adventure, by a *deus ex machina* in a grey-blue uniform and a couple of tin derbies" (p. 7). Cummings would probably have been freed after his initial interrogation if he had cooperated in the way his questioners thought that he should. When he refused to say that he hated the Germans, though, he was further detained. Asked the question *"Est-ce que vous détes-tez les boches?"*, he insisted on answering *"Non. J'aime beaucoup les français"* (p. 19). He ultimately spent almost three months in a French prison, really a concentration camp where "suspicious" persons could be detained on no specific charge.

It was largely due to his father's efforts that he was released in December, 1917, and it was primarily due to his father's insistence that he finally wrote about his experiences in the French prison. Cummings wanted to sail back to Europe in 1920. Instead, he wrote *The Enormous Room* in a tree-house at Hurricane Point that he and his father had built. It was first published in 1922 and had a very mixed reception. On the one hand, it was hailed as an unrivaled masterpiece, a veritable *tour de force*; on the other, it was denounced as indecent and unpatriotic. It is today generally accepted as an important statement on human freedom and injustice.

Cummings was not yet finished with the war, however. He returned to New York shortly after he was released from prison in France, but had only a short stay. In the summer of 1918 he was drafted and ordered to Camp Devens, Massachusetts. He reported there and was trained as an infantry soldier until the Armistice. Brown was also drafted after he got out of prison, but the scurvy he had contracted in prison had left him in such bad health that he was discharged as soon as he arrived at camp.

Cummings' brief experience at Camp Devens served to confirm what *La Ferté Macé* had taught him. The effect was decisive and certainly played an important role in reshaping some of his values. He had never had a great deal of use for authoritarian dogma; after his war experience, he knew positive reasons for opposing it. If the individual and the underdog were inside the prisons as victims of the system, then the system was not only "wrong," it should be actively opposed. The poems which were to come from Cummings were going to be in part an opposition to an increasingly authoritarian society.

With Brown, he took a studio in New York after the Armistice. He spent the next two years there, painting and writing. He became part of the New York remembered by Dos Passos as being an emanation of Cambridge. He and Elaine Orr, who was to become his first wife, were the hub of a circle composed mainly of people who had known each other at Harvard. It was in some ways a rather inbred circle; Elaine had earlier been married to Scofield Thayer who, along with Sibley Watson, was to edit the new *Dial* for nine and a half years, from January, 1920, to July 1929.

The stimulus of being in New York led to Cummings' becoming known as something of a conversationalist. The following description of an evening in Cummings' company is typical:

> After a couple of brandies on top of the wine Cummings would deliver himself of geysers of talk. I've never heard anything that remotely approached it. It was comical ironical learned brilliantlycolored intricately cadenced damnably poetic and sometimes just naughty. It was as if he were spouting pages of prose and verse from an unwritten volume. Then suddenly he would go off to

Patchin Place to put some of it down before the fountain ceased to flow.

His mind was essentially extemporaneous. His fits of poetic fury were like the maenadic seizures described in Greek lyrics. . . .

Those New York nights none of us wanted to waste time at the theater when there was a chance that Cummings might go off like a stack of Roman candles after dinner. (John Dos Passos, *The Best Times*, pp. 83–84)

Cummings must have taken nights off, however, for there were plenty of evenings at theaters of various sorts:

Then nearby there was always the classical burlesque show upstairs in the building at the end of the avenue. We claimed that Minsky's was in the direct line from Aristophanes, and Terence and Plautus. After the circus, which was his favorite show, Cummings in those days esteemed burlesque. We were late getting to bed the nights. . . . (*The Best Times*, pp. 84–85)

Cummings played hard during those years; he also worked hard and traveled a lot. He appeared in the first issue of the new *Dial.* He wrote and continued to work on *The Enormous Room.* In 1921 he traveled to Portugal and Spain with Dos Passos, then to Paris, which became his European headquarters for the next two years. He spent part of 1922 in Italy, then returned to France, where he remained until the autumn of 1923, when he returned to New York, this time to the apartment at Patchin Place which would remain his address until his death. There he continued with the painting and writing which had become his life in Europe.

The Enormous Room was, as we noted earlier, greeted by a mixed reception when it appeared in 1922; but many reviews were perceptive ones. Those critics who objected to the language of the book and its strong tone of disgust failed to take into account an important mood of disenchantment in the United States after the war. Cummings was not the only writer who found the war brutal. Other books which dealt with the whole dreary story and its sordid settlement were Sir Philip Gibbs's *Now It Can Be Told* and *More That Must Be Told*, John Maynard Keynes's *Economic Consequences of the Peace*, and, in fiction, John Dos Passos' *Three Soldiers*. Dos Passos wrote a very delightful and perceptive review in 1922:

31

Here's a book that has been conceived unashamedly and directly without a thought either of the colmunists or the book trade or Mr Sumner, or of fitting neatly into any one of the neatly labelled pigeonholes of novel, play, essay, history, travel book, a book that exists because the author was so moved, excited, amused by a certain slice of his existence that things happened freely and cantankerously on paper. And he had the nerve to let things happen. In this pattern-cut generation, most writers are too afraid of losing their private reputations as red-blooded clear-eyed hundred-percenters, well-dressed, well-mannered and thoroughly disinfected fashion plates, to make any attempt to feel and express directly the life about them and in them. They walk in daily fear that someone will call them morbid, and insulate themselves from their work with the rubber raincoat of fiction. *The Enormous Room* seems to me to be the book that has nearest approached the mood of reckless adventure in which men will reach the white heat of imagination needed to fuse the soggy disjointed complexity of the industrial life about us into seething fluid of creation. There can be no more playing safe. Like the old steamboat captains on the Mississippi we'll have to forget the hissing of the safety-valve and stoke like beavers if we are to get off the sticky shoals into the deeper reaches beyond. And many an old tub will blow sky high with all hands before someone makes the course. *The Enormous Room* for one seems to me to have cleared the shoals. ("Off the Shoals," *The Dial*, LXXIII, July, 1922, pp. 98–99. Reprinted in Baum, pp. 4–5)

The following year, as I've said, his first full volume of poetry appeared. *Tulips and Chimneys* was important as much for the range of *kinds* of poems it contained as for some of the poems themselves. There were experiments. One style that Cummings was clearly developing made extensive use of lower-case, unusual typographical arrangements, and punctuational gymnastics. If one recalls the offended critics and howls of outrage which greeted these early experiments, it is particularly interesting to note that that first volume opened with a poem—"Epithalamion"—of twenty-one eight-line rhymed stanzas, and ended with seventeen sonnets, several of which are regularly included in any contemporary anthology of poetry which devotes more than a page to the poetry of Cummings.

Some readers, of course, were already familiar with the poems he had published in various periodicals. By far the most important of these periodicals was *The Dial*. The journal transformed by Thayer and Watson was not the original publication by that name, the one founded in the nineteenth century by Margaret Fuller and Ralph Waldo Emerson, but a continuation of a re-established *Dial* which was moved to New York City in 1917. It suffered financial difficulties soon after being moved to New York, and it was soon sold to Thayer and Watson, who had been at Harvard with Cummings. They transformed it into a truly remarkable publication, one which contained a great deal more about art than any other publication in America. The first issue contained writings by Paul Rosenfeld, Edwin Arlington Robinson, Maxwell Bodenheim, Carl Sandburg, Evelyn Scott, Walter Pach, and of course E. E. Cummings, who was represented by seven poems and four line drawings.

It was the beginning of a long and mutually satisfactory relationship between Cummings and *The Dial*. Cummings was a frequent contributor throughout the life of the publication; all told, the *Dial* published thirty-seven of his poems, several critical articles, parts of the play *Him*, and numerous drawings and paintings. He was absolutely unknown in 1920; by 1929, when the *Dial* ceased publication, he had published four volumes of poems plus *The Enormous Room* and *Him*.

The height of the *Dial's* support came, of course, in 1926, when it was announced that Cummings had been given the Dial Award for 1925. An extremely prestigious award, it had previously gone to Sherwood Anderson (1921), T. S. Eliot (for *The Waste Land*, 1922), Van Wyck Brooks (1923), and Marianne Moore (for *Observations*, 1924). The award, in the amount of $2000, was specifically for "proved merit" and "distinguished service to American letters." The announcement naming Cummings as the recipient mentioned *The Enormous Room*, *Tulips and Chimneys*, *XLI Poems*, and & *[AND]*. Watson's announcement was the occasion for his statement that he feared it would be about seventy years before criticism would begin to "come up with" Cummings' verse; he hoped to speed things along. Possibly he did; it was only about two decades before Cummings' poems reached a general audience in America. During those two decades, Cummings produced six more volumes of poems.

Cummings' relationship with *The Dial* was a special one. He was regarded by the editors as their arch-discovery; not so gener-

ally recognized is the esteem in which Cummings held the journal.
A recent history of *The Dial* tells us that

> Among contributors themselves, only E. E. Cummings, whom
> Pound calls *The Dial's* white-haired boy, is wholehearted in his
> respect for the journal and his affection for its editors. (*The Time
> of the DIAL*, p. 168)

It was during his years with *The Dial* that Cummings acquired
the reputation of being the *enfant terrible* of American letters.
Why he should have been the one modern figure sponsored absolutely without reserve by the editors of *The Dial* is not really
known, but it is true that he was considered such a characteristic
contributor that Thayer once closed the pages of that publication
to J. Middleton Murry after Murry wrote an essay disparaging
Cummings' poetry. "Feeling as you do about the work of so
important and characteristic a contributor to *The Dial* as Mr
Cummings, I should not think you would care to write further for
The Dial," he said (*The Time of the DIAL*, p. 90). The respect in
which Cummings' productions were held was not confined to his
literary productions. Another historian has documented for us the
fact that

> The only abstract painting that comes to mind as having been
> reproduced in *The Dial* is E. E. Cummings' *Noise Number 13*, re-
> produced to accompany the selections from *Him*. It may well be
> that such a picture appeared because of the unusual editorial leni-
> ency towards Cummings, who was, wrote Alfred Kreymborg, *The
> Dial's* arch-discovery. (*Scofield Thayer and THE DIAL*, p. 224)

The publication of the selections from *Him* was itself noteworthy. The only other dramatic piece printed by *The Dial* (and
later reviewed when it was produced) was Leonid Andreyev's *He,
the One Who Gets Slapped*, in Gregory Zilhourg's translation (later
published by *The Dial* as a pamphlet).

The respect was mutual. As Dos Passos further recorded,

> Except for the people on the *Dial*, whom he considered old
> friends, Cummings was leery of wasting his days with editors and
> publishers. He never pretended to be practical about practical
> matters. He thought a poet should be fed by the ravens, and of
> course he was. (*The Best Times*, p. 85)

Dos Passos' comment should be taken with a grain of salt—he has admitted that in his own case the ravens proved neglectful—and it should be noted that the Dial Award increased both Cummings' prestige and prosperity, though not to the extent that the editors would probably have liked.

The year 1926 was for Cummings both a good and a bad year. His fourth volume, *is 5*, appeared early in the year. Later in the year, his father was killed in an automobile accident which also left his mother seriously injured. The courage with which she rallied after the tragic event probably served as the immediate inspiration for the poem in which Cummings expressed his love and admiration for her. The poem, "if there are any heavens my mother will (all by herself) have," appeared in his next published volume, *W [ViVa]*, in 1931.

Cummings later wrote a poetic tribute to his father. The poem, "my father moved through dooms of love," was published in *50 Poems* (1940). It is justifiably one of the best-known and most popular of Cummings' poems. It reflects the understanding gratitude he felt toward his father for being the man he was. In particular, it reminds the reader familiar with Cummings' life of the efforts of the elder Cummings to get him released from prison during the war.

Cummings made several short trips to Europe during the twenties, the first of them to Paris in 1924. Upon his return to New York after that trip, he once more got a job, this time one more suited to his life-style than the one he had had working for Collier. He had a roving assignment for *Vanity Fair* which left him free to travel, as he continued to do frequently through the twenties and into the thirties.

In 1927 Cummings married for the second time. His first marriage to Elaine Orr, mother of his only child Nancy, had ended earlier. His marriage to Anne Barton, previously married to Ralph Barton, a caricaturist, was also to end in divorce. Little is recorded about those first two marriages. Apparently none of the letters Cummings wrote his first two wives has survived. He and Nancy, who was brought up under another name, established a close relationship only after she was a young woman. Though Cummings apparently saw her frequently when she was a very young child, there was a hiatus in their relationship. Norman suggests that the play *Santa Claus* contains, in poetic and symbolic form, some autobiographical elements of Cummings' own life, one of which involves a little girl recognizing Santa Claus (who has exchanged masks with Death), but failing to realize that he is also her father.

Beginning that same year, Cummings directed some of his energies to drama. His first play, *Him*, grew rapidly. In August of 1927 *The Dial* published six scenes from the play, and the entire work was published later the same year. Produced the following year in New York by the Provincetown Players, under the direction of James Light, it ran for six weeks, during which time the critics and reviewers had a field day, while audiences filled the little theater. A persistent deficit (the production cost more than $6000, while the average expenditure on Provincetown plays was $2000, finally closed it down.

There were indications that Cummings planned to continue writing plays. In its 1928–1929 announcement, the Provincetown said that he was writing a second play, but it was never produced. However, in 1930 Cummings wrote a short one-act play, *Anthropos: The Future of Art*, which appeared first in a symposium entitled *Whither, Whither, or After Sex, What? A Symposium to End Symposiums*, and was then published separately in a limited edition. In 1930 a collection of nonsense fairy-tales, bearing no title, also appeared.

The year 1931 was a big one for Cummings, and it began for him a rich and productive decade. He made the trip to Russia which was to form the subject matter of his second full-length prose work, *Eimi*. He had his first major showing of paintings, twenty-nine pictures exhibited at the Painters and Sculptors Gallery. He published *CIOPW*, a collection of works done in charcoal, ink, oil, pencil, and watercolor. *W [ViVa]* was published.

Then in 1932 he met and married Marion Morehouse, well-known as a model, an actress, and a photographer. Edward Steichen once said of her that she was the best fashion model he had ever worked with. She has for many years been well known for her photographs of Cummings. The volume *Adventures in Value*, an album of fifty photographs published shortly before her death, demonstrates the range of her photographic interests. From the time she and Cummings met, they were rarely apart. Their closeness is attested in many ways; for instance, he dedicated four volumes to her during his lifetime.

That same year there were two New York exhibitions of Cummings' paintings.

In 1933 he made a trip to Europe and Tunisia as the holder of a Guggenheim Fellowship. And *Eimi* was published, announced as a novel. It is not, of course, any such thing, but a kind of diary whose unique feature is constant evocation of the immediacy of experience and realization. It is as much in a class by itself as was *The Enormous Room*. There are certain similarities between the two books, but of the two *Eimi* is the more difficult to read. It had few readers in its early printings; that was as much because of *what* it said as *how* it said it. For it appeared at the "wrong" time. In 1933 many American intellectuals, convinced that the Soviet Union could do no wrong, felt that nothing done anywhere else could be right. It has always seemed ironic that Cummings, one of the few American writers of his time to completely reject Marxism, was also one of the few who actually traveled to Russia. Ezra Pound once suggested that when Russia was interesting, Cummings had gone there, and that others who wanted to know about Russia to the extent that Cummings wanted to might do well to show like activity.

Cummings was never sympathetic to the program of the Communist Party, either in Russia or in the United States. He apparently felt that that fact was responsible for his being without a publisher at this time in his life. His most recent collection of poems, eventually published as *No Thanks*, made the round of a number of publishers, each of whom declined to publish it. Why a sixth volume of poems by a writer as well-established as Cummings was should be rejected by fourteen major publishers is not known. Whatever the reason, the result might have been that a poet of Cummings' stature was denied an audience. Fortunately, he was not. Cummings finally issued the book himself, with the financial assistance of his mother, to whom the terminal dedication is made. An initial dedication follows the title and is to

Farrar & Rhinehart
Simon & Schuster
Coward-McCann
Limited Editions

Harcourt, Brace
Random House
Equinox Press
Smith & Haas
Viking Press
Knopf
Dutton
Harper's
Scribner's
Covici, Friede

It was published by Samuel A. Jacobs at the Golden Eagle Press in three limited editions. There was first a holograph edition of nine copies, each priced at $99. Subscribers were assured that a poem in holograph, No. 44, would never be printed. A De Luxe issue of ninety copies omitted Poem 44, as did the first trade edition of nine hundred copies. Subsequent trade editions of the volume have a blank page where this poem should be, and there is a blank page (except for the poem's number) in *Poems 1923–1954* and the trade edition of the 1968 *Complete Poems*. The poem is available in the De Luxe edition of the 1968 *Complete Poems* and also in the trade edition of the 1972 *Complete Poems*. The 1938 *Collected Poems* (recently re-issued) simply omitted any mention of the poem. The book, a very good one, is full of invention and continued experimentation. Most notable, perhaps, is the "grasshopper" poem, "r-p-o-p-h-e-s-a-g-r," which continues alternately to grieve and to delight its readers. The book also contained a number of sonnets.

During 1935 Cummings also published *Tom*, a ballet based on *Uncle Tom's Cabin*. Although it was never staged, David Diamond composed a complete score for it. This work was apparently suggested by Marion Morehouse to whom Cummings gives credit in the dedication.

It should be remembered that Cummings' work during and after the period of the Depression was greatly influenced by the difficulties and hardships of that time. He himself had financial difficulties for much of his adult life, and they were rendered even more severe by the economic situation in America in the late twenties and the early thirties. But more important than his personal situation was his growing awareness that many of his fellow

Americans were willing to do almost anything for what they called "security," not realizing just exactly how high a price one pays for it. Cummings was not willing to pay for "security"; one apparent result was that he remained without a publisher in his own country until 1938. In 1936, however, there was published *1/20* [*One over Twenty*], the first volume of his poems to be published in Britain. It was published by Contemporary Poetry and Prose Editions, London.

There was another trip to Paris during 1937, during which year Cummings also published the Archetype Edition of *Tulips & Chimneys* and arranged for the publication of the incorrectly titled *Collected Poems*, which appeared in 1938, published by Harcourt, Brace. The jacket of the first edition of *Collected Poems* states:

> Mr Cummings has written a score of new poems and an Introduction for this collection. In addition, he has included in this book all of the poems from his earlier books—"Tulips and Chimneys," "And," "XLI Poems," "Is Five," "Viva," and "No Thanks"—which he wishes to preserve.

There were 315 poems in the book, including twenty-two new ones. Some favorites are missing; they were collected in *Poems 1923–1954* and in the British and American editions of *Complete Poems*. Another new volume, *50 Poems*, appeared in 1940, the year in which Cummings received an award from the Academy of American Poets.

There was war again, and Cummings' writings reflect the state of the world. Many of the poems in *1 x 1* (1944) reflect his preoccupation with the evils of the world, evils which are apparently never going to be solved by war. Even before the entry of the United States into the war, the country was affected by it, and one immediate result was the beginning of a period of war-time boom that was finally to end the bread-lines of the depression. By February, 1940, *Fortune Magazine*, celebrating *its* first decade, was able to exult that October, 1939, the tenth anniversary of the Wall Street crash, had marked the end of a ten-year industrial depression. Even though some nine million Americans were still unemployed, that figure represented a decline in the number who had been unemployed during the preceding decade—the figure had

been as high as fifteen million at one point. Defense work brought
about a swift and dramatic change in the economy; war factories
began to operate three shifts, and incomes soared as the work
week lengthened. Man does not live by his standard of living alone,
however, and war-time prosperity was accompanied by unpleasant
side-effects, some of which had particular relevance to a poet and
artist. A letter written by Cummings late in 1940 tells of his
concern over what was happening in American life:

> the poet Hart Crane would thunder there'd always been and would
> always remain three sorts of people: warriors,priests,merchants. I
> imagine an artist(whatever his art)is a kind of priest,or perhaps vice
> versa;no artist surely is a moneymaker and no artist surely is a man-
> killer. Also perhaps:if enough skindeep socalledpeople are so con-
> fused about what they are that they'd itch rather than not be what
> they aren't,this socalledworld will change hisher skin
>
> also surely:if nobody ever escapes with something(e.g. I avoided the
> American army,by visiting France with a Norton Harjes ambulance
> unit,merely to have myself drafted later and serve six months at
> Camp Devens)only whatever is artificial perishes (*Selected Letters*,
> pp. 157–158)

The volume of poems written during the war years became the
second one by Cummings to be published in Britain. Largely due
to the efforts of Cyril Connolly, editor of *Horizon* and a long-time
admirer of Cummings' poetry, the volume *1 x 1* was published in
1947, at the Horizon Press. It was a beautiful book, bound in
yellow and containing an introduction by Lloyd Frankenberg. It
was published on Cummings' fifty-third birthday, October 14.
Cummings himself was quite pleased with the book; its reception
was not, however, kind. It annoyed many reviewers, and probably
puzzled many more. Some reviewers simply returned the book un-
read.

Cummings had exhibitions in both 1944 and 1945. There was
a show of oils and watercolors at the American British Art Gallery
in New York in 1944, and a show of oils, watercolors, and sketches
in Rochester in 1945.

Two events of special interest in Cummings' life occurred simultaneously in 1946. The Spring issue of *The Harvard Wake* that
year was a special "Cummings Number," and contained in it was

a new play, *Santa Claus* (subtitled A Morality). The issue also contained two other works by Cummings himself, a fairy tale and a poem, and an impressive collection of tributes by other writers. William Carlos Williams praised Cummings' achievement in language, pointing to what he took to be the inherently Christian quality of a language which addresses the private conscience of each of us in turn. With admirable economy, Marianne Moore concluded her brief note with the starkly simple statement that Cummings did not make "aesthetic mistakes." Theodore Spencer took the opportunity to make some observations on the nature of Cummings' most recent poems, pointing out that they were marked by sharper satire, an original sense of rhythm, and deepened emotional subject matter. Allen Tate paid tribute in the form of a latter to Cummings which he wrote for publication in the *Wake*. The body of it read as follows:

> What I am about to say will sound like irony because no man should be praised for the minimum performance of his obligation as a human being, which is to remain human; and no poet deserves praise for remaining a poet. Yet in looking back over the war years I see only one American poet who kept his humanity and his poetry, and that man is Estlin Cummings. I don't want to be unjust to anybody else; I am talking about my generation and my friends; there may be younger men who behaved honorably as men and poets. Among the men of our age some kept their humanity, some their poetry; but none, I think, both. (p. 30)

Contributions praising Cummings came from many of America's leading writers: Lionel Trilling, Jacques Barzun, Paul Rosenfeld and others. John Dos Passos had this to say:

> So few people, especially among those who make it their business to write about writing, seem to think of writing as a special skill, like the skill of a fisherman, or a farmer or an experimental chemist, that it's not surprising that after twenty years they are still telling us about the oddities of E. E. Cummings' work. To his contemporaries who have followed roughly similar occupations it's his skill that has been so continually stimulating. The oddities are a side issue. Anyway, good English writing, notably at times when there was need to deal with some fundamentally fresh aspect of life, has been full of oddities. They are a by-product of originality. Originality is the cast of mind that is bound at all costs to deal with each fresh

41

event as if it had never been dealt with before. It is only the original cast of mind that ever discovers or invents anything. To my way of thinking Cummings is, within his field of personal emotion, the lyrical field, one of the inventors of our time. He puts his inventions down with an unexpected refurbishing of phrase and a filigree delicacy of hair-breadth exact statement that is a continual challenge and incitement to other writers. I certainly don't think that the workmanlike skill shown in the poems, in *The Enormous Room*, or in the shrewd odd annoyingly sound account of his trip to Russia that he called *Eimi*, is going to be any less stimulating as time goes on. (p. 64)

Cummings' mother died in 1947. He was not to outlive her by many years. Nevertheless, he continued to write and to paint and in May, 1949, had a show of watercolors, oils, and drawings at the American British Art Center.

Then in 1950 appeared *Xaipe*, the last single volume to appear before the great collection, *Poems 1923–1954*. In that year, Cummings was awarded a Fellowship of the Academy of American Poets for "great achievement." He spent part of the year abroad, travelling to France, Italy, and Greece.

The critical reception of *Xaipe* was, as usual with Cummings' works, varied. Increasingly, it had become clear that for all their differences, Cummings' admirers and his detractors agreed in finding his poetry "different." What some of these differences are — and are not—will be examined in detail further in this work. At this point, however, it is interesting to note that Cummings' poetry was beginning to attract the serious attention of men in disciplines quite different from his own. One reviewer of *Xaipe*, for instance, was Donald H. Andrews, a professor of chemistry at Johns Hopkins University. Professor Hopkins praised Cummings as an innovator in the difficult art of communication and suggested that far from being either obscure or affected, Cummings' poems have a high density of meaning and are the result of a process whereby there is a constant transformation of dimension from idea to eye, from eye to ear, and from both to subconscious association. The result is a new language. (*The Hopkins Review*, Summer, 1950)

In 1951 Cummings was again awarded a Guggenheim Fellowship. His Aunt Jane died that year also, and left him a small in-

heritance. These events eased somewhat the financial strain
which he had lived most of his life. His selection as Charles
Norton Professor of Poetry at Harvard University for the acad
year 1952–1953 helped to ease the strain further.

It also resulted in an enormous personal success. Cummings
delivered six lectures at Harvard during the 1952–1953 school
year. The first lecture, on October 28, was delivered to a packed
Sanders Theatre. By the third lecture, there was standing room
only; the door to Sanders Theatre was locked, and more than fifty
students were turned away. Many of them protested vigorously
outside the door, before they finally left.

Cummings had written the lectures during the summer of 1952.
They were published in 1953 by Harvard University Press, under
the title *i:six nonlectures*. In the lectures Cummings reviewed his
entire life, indicating what he believed to have been the formative
influences. In addition he included an anthology of passages from
his own work, prose as well as poetry, and from the work of
Wordsworth, Nashe, Chaucer, Swinburne, Charles d'Orleans,
Shakespeare, Catullus, Horace, Sappho, Dante, Robert Burns, Wal-
ther von der Vogelweide, Keats, and Shelley. All readings were in
the original. Also included were several ballads from Child's collection.

Nothing has been said thus far about Cummings as a reader.
He did give a number of readings during his lifetime. He was, for
instance, the first poet to read at the Poetry Centre of the
Y.M.H.A., Lexington Avenue at 92nd Street, New York City. He
sometimes read there to audiences overflowing into the aisles; indeed, it was often his experience that vast and unexpected crowds
awaited him when he arrived to give a reading. Once when he went
to Bennington College in Vermont to give a reading, he was almost
literally bowled over by his reception. As he walked up the stairs
to the top floor of the Commons Building, he heard the students
chanting the words of "Buffalo Bill's/defunct" (I, 60). When he
walked onto the platform, the girls rose and continued chanting
in unison. He waved his handkerchief; the girls then cheered.

The readings given during his later years were a concession to
the public and to his need for money. They were given in all parts
of the country, mostly to college audiences. They required a deliberate relaxation of his demand for privacy and also a great deal of

physical courage, for he was partly crippled by arthritis and so wore a brace on his back that jutted out two inches from his shoulder blades. He had to read sitting on a straight-backed kitchen chair. Nonetheless, students flocked to his readings through his last years. An account by Malcolm Cowley indicates that the crowds at Sanders Theatre in 1952–1953 were not isolated phenomena. Cowley heard him read at the University of Michigan in 1957. The hall in which Cummings was reading had eight hundred seats, and, according to Cowley, was full long before the reading began. After the doors were locked, more than a thousand students milled about outside. Cowley said it was the first and last time in the United States that he had heard of students almost rioting to hear a poetry reading. As he pointed out, Cummings must have enjoyed that tribute to the magic of his verse.

The excitement of such a literary performance can never be captured in its entirety on a recording, though it is of course the next best thing for those who did not hear Cummings read during his lifetime. The recordings of the Harvard "nonlectures" are of particular interest, for they were made live at Sanders Theatre. Available also are recordings of a number of readings from his own works and these are listed in the Bibliographical Note. The seriousness with which he tackled these ventures is exemplified by an excerpt from Lloyd Frankenberg's account of his attempt to put together *Pleasure Dome: an audible anthology of modern poetry.*

> Cummings left the engineers flabbergasted, with a tape they'd marked as trial. Timed to the split'second, it was played back. "You can't," said Cummings with an accolade to the staff, "improve on perfection." (*Pleasure Dome*, p. 16)

The first full collection of Cummings' poems, *Poems 1923–1954*, was not published until 1954—the earlier *Collected Poems* (1938) had been a selection, rather than a proper edition. And three volumes had been published since 1938. So the *Poems 1923–1954*, as published by Harcourt, Brace and Company, was a welcome if somewhat overdue occurrence. Even it had an inaccurate title, however, for it included no poems written after 1950. This resulted from a misunderstanding between Cummings and the editorial office of Harcourt, Brace. The one originally suggested by the poet was *Poems 1923–1950*. However, he did sign a contract in which the latter date appeared as 1954.

The volume contains a total of 598 poems, from the following sources: *Tulips and Chimneys* (1923), *& [AND]* (1925), *XLI Poems* (1925), *Is 5* (1926), *W [ViVa]* (1931), *No Thanks* (1935), *"New Poems,"* from *Collected Poems* (1938), *50 Poems* (1940), *1 x 1* (1944), and *Xaipe* (1950). It also contains, in the Table of Contents, a complete listing (in order of appearance in the volume) of the first lines of all the untitled poems. It is an important item, since practically all the poems are untitled.

Again, critical response was varied—if, by now, a bit predictable. Many critics expressed their pleasure in the availability of the poems in a single volume. Others were quick to point out that the collection would have been better for some pruning. The most perceptive critics were those who recognized the importance of Cummings' late satire. Louise Bogan's review for *The New Yorker* (XXX, December 11, 1954, pp. 198–202) was significant for its insights into Cummings' growth as a poet, saying that he had

brought into American postwar poetry a bittersweet mixture of satire and sentiment. His typographical experiments, which gave him an early notoriety, today seem less important than his persistent attempts to break taboos—to bring back into formal verse material that Victorian taste had outlawed. Today, as we read Cummings' lyric output from beginning to end, we are struck by the directness with which he has presented himself—his adolescent daydreams as well as his more mature desires; his small jealousies and prejudices, along with his big hatreds; his negative malice and his fears, beside his positive hopes. His awareness of tradition, too, comes out plainly; he has reworked traditional forms as often as he has invented new ones, turning not only the sonnet to his own purposes but also the ballad, the nursery rhyme, the epigrammatic quatrain, and the incantatory rune. . . . But it is his satire that remains focal and sharp as his main contribution to the reinvigoration of modern verse. His targets have been, for the most part, well chosen, and he has made his stand clear—for the rights and value of the individual as opposed to the demands of the crowd and the standards of the machine. It is this underlying passion for simple justice that has given Cummings the power to uncover, point to, and stigmatize those dead areas of custom as only a satirist can effectively do it. (pp. 198, 201)

45

Another point of view was expressed by Randall Jarrell, who reviewed the collection for *The New York Times Book Review* on October 31, 1954. In the review, entitled "A Poet's Own Way," Jarrell questioned Cummings' rank as a poet and suggested that the collection was more a picnic than a feast:

> It's a picnic which has its points—and what would life be without picnics? What I'm objecting to is calling it a Lucullan feast and Cummings the American Brillat-Savarin. "E. E. Cummings has achieved a permanent place among the great poets of this age," says his dust-jacket; has he, or has he a place all his own, among the good poets of the age? If Cummings is a great poet, what are you going to call Eliot and Frost? Rilke? Let's say together: "Great me no greats," and leave this grading to posterity. (p. 6)

In the event, it was perhaps better to leave the grading to posterity. For one thing, Cummings was still writing, and the last years of his life were as productive as earlier years. That productivity was recognized in 1955 when he received a special citation by the National Book Award for *Poems 1923–1954*.

In 1956 the poet made a trip to Europe, visiting Spain, Italy, and France.

In 1957 he received the prestigious Bollingen Prize in Poetry and also the Boston Arts Festival Poetry Award. At that festival he gave a public reading, the history of which sheds light on the interesting and complex relationship between Cummings and establishment acadamicians. When Cummings was invited to be Festival Poet at the Boston Arts Festival in June, he was told that the only stipulation was that he agree to read a poem specifically for the occasion; additionally, he would be asked to read from his poems, preferably with commentary, for an hour or so one evening. Following some initial disagreements about what a "Festival Poem" should be, Cummings accepted the invitation. Eventually, Peter Temple, manager of the Festival, asked for a copy of the Festival poem, so that it could be released to the Boston newspapers in advance of the actual reading. Obligingly, Cummings sent two copies of "Thanksgiving (1956)," a poem occasioned by the recent events in Hungary, and one which is noteworthy for its personification of America in the form of Uncle Sam responding to Hungary's cry for help. It concludes thus:

uncle sam shrugs his pretty
pink shoulders you know how
and he twitches a liberal titty
and lisps "i'm busy right now"

so rah-rah-rah democracy
let's all be thankful as hell
and bury the statue of liberty
(because it begins to smell)
(II, 711)

There was a long silence; finally, rumor reached Cummings that the poem he had sent would not be acceptable as a Festival poem. On May 21, he telegraphed his withdrawal as Festival poet. He was persuaded to reconsider, but it remained clear that the Festival Committee did not consider the submitted poem suitable to the occasion. Again, he reconsidered, this time deciding that he would read as the Festival poem another new poem that he had previously considered for the occasion. However, he announced that he would *also* read "Thanksgiving (1956)," and indeed he did. It was received warmly by the crowd of seven thousand who heard him read. Many people doubtless thought it ironic that the Festival poem was "i am a little church (no great cathedral)" (II, 749), a very Christian poem which is strongly reminiscent, in tone and message, of the section of the Old English poem "The Dream of the Rood" in which the rood, or cross, on which Christ was slain, explains to the world his feeling about serving in such a position.

In 1958 Cummings had two books published, *A Miscellany*, a collection of fugitive pieces, and *95 Poems*, his first collection of new poems since *Xaipe*, and two years later he made his final trip abroad, this time to Italy, Greece, and France.

Shortly before his death, Cummings and his wife had begun making plans to move from their Greenwich Village address. He had loved his years in New York, but the city and his neighborhood had changed over the years from the wonderfully stimulating place he had first found it to be. In fact, the New York City of 1960 was at least as different from the New York City of 1917—the date Cummings first encountered it—as the New York City of 1917 was from the Boston that Cummings moved so far away from during his life. He had decided to divide his remaining years

47

between the Joy Farm in New Hampshire and Europe. He and Marion had long spent a part of each year on the farm. Now they were making plans to spend six months a year there. Electricity was being installed, and arrangements for adequate heating were being made. Then on September 3, 1962, he collapsed of a cerebral hemorrhage at Joy Farm.

The tributes came thick and fast, most of them praising his innovations. *The New York Times* called him a "magnificent poet." In its one-page tribute, *Time* magazine refrained from ranking him —suggesting that it is no easier to compare poets than it is to compare peaches and blueberries—and concluded, with Archibald MacLeish, that "there are very few people who deserve the word poet. Cummings was one of them." The tribute Cummings might have enjoyed most was recounted on a back page of *The New York Times* the day following his death:

> "He was the third beautiful person to die this year," one waitress was telling another in the Van Dyck Food Shop at 270 West Forty-third Street yesterday.
>
> "Who died?" a patron asked over the counter.
>
> "Cummings. I heard it on the radio. He was born in 1894. He died today," she replied.
>
> "E. E. Cummings? He died? Do you like Cummings?"
>
> "in Just-/ spring when the world is mud-/ luscious the little/ lame balloonman/ whistles far and wee," she recited. "I have two of his books."
>
> "Yes, I have a book of his," the other waitress interjected. "He was nice."
>
> "Who else beautiful died this year?" the patron asked.
>
> "Kovacs," the first waitress replied. "Ernie Kovacs and Marilyn Monroe. And Cummings. I think they were beautiful people. They all died."

Later in 1962 there appeared a book published jointly by Cummings and his wife, *Adventures in Value*; Marion Morehouse took the photographs, while Cummings wrote the text for it.

The following year a new collection, *73 Poems*, was published posthumously. It was followed in 1965 by *A Miscellany Revised*, an expended edition of the 1958 volume, and *Fairy Tales*, illustrated by John Eaton.

There have been three important publications since then. First, there are now available complete editions of the poetry. In 1968 *Complete Poems* was published by MacGibbon and Kee, London. The first volume includes poems written 1913–1935; the second, poems written 1936–1962. It was published in two editions, one a numbered, limited edition which contains a facsimile reproduction of Poem 44 of *No Thanks*. The set is a particularly handsome collection, its main virtue—other than completeness—being that it restores to the poems Cummings' preferred arrangement of never including two poems or parts of poems on the same page. This was a principle strictly adhered to in his individual volumes; both *Collected Poems* (1938) and *Poems 1923–1954* (1954), however, had been designed to reduce the number of pages required by using all available space on each page. An important item is an alphabetical Index of First Lines, a tool never before available to the general reader. In 1972 a similar edition, in one volume, was published by Harcourt, Brace, Jovanovich, Inc., New York.

Some of Cummings' letters are now available. Edited by F. W. Dupee and George Stade, *Selected Letters of E. E. Cummings* was published by Harcourt, Brace and World in 1969 and includes letters from 1899 to 1962. It is particularly enlightening for the reader who wants to know something more about Cummings the man than one can learn from either knowing his works or reading a brief biography. He was an interesting and complex figure, a man capable of great gentleness, but one who could on occasion be quite haughty. Above all, he was a man to whom his own taste mattered more than anything else. Consequently, he sometimes expressed great contempt for those who seemed to him to have no taste. As he grew older, he was sometimes accused of intolerance. Ironically, he *was* intolerant; the irony of his intolerance was once commented on by his friend Dos Passos, who acknowledged its existence and watched its development:

> A phase we had in common of this same private cult was an off-hand downunderneath reverence toward the idosyncrasy of the divergent, various, incalculable men, women, and children who make up the human race. As Cummings grew older, he narrowed it down. Tolerance is not a New England vice. I never shared his intolerance. He had the brahmin's disdain for anyone who didn't live up to certain specifications.

> "Dead from the neck up," he called them; but in some of what

seem to me to be his best poems, and in the descriptions of people in *The Enormous Room*, he expressed better than I was ever able to express them, feelings of mine about men seen in bitter moments at the front, or among the black tents of the Bedaii: the incongruous splendor, the spark of God—how else can I say it?—I sought in every human clod. (*The Best Times*, p. 134)

Further evidence of a haughty and biting side can be found in some of the published letters; in one, for instance, he suggests to a correspondent who has sent him a manuscript that he "learn to write English," since it's "one of the more beautiful languages" (*Selected Letters*, p. 205). He could also be quite generous with his help, however; many of the published letters are painstakingly detailed explications of poems about which he had received questions from puzzled readers.

Marion Morehouse died of cancer on May 18, 1969, after a long illness. Until her death, however, she remained active in aiding and encouraging students and writers. Her devotion to Cummings and his work had not been passive.

These are, in brief, the external events of the life of E. E. Cummings. The external events which have been dealt with in this chapter were not, however, the most real events of his life. These were the internal events, the ones that happened in his mind and took form as the poems and other writings that he published, as well as the paintings that he did. It is those things with which the rest of this volume is concerned.

2
Early Poetry

It is easy to believe Cummings' statement: "I did not decide to become a poet—I was always writing poetry." For vast quantities of early unpublished writing—much of it in verse—survive in manuscript. The two couplets quoted earlier are probably his earliest surviving poetic attempts, but hundreds of other unpublished poems survive from the years 1902–1916, from his eighth to his twenty-second years. Although few of them are particularly good, they are important because they demonstrate the discipline involved in Cummings' mastery of the *craft* of poetry—for long periods during those years he must have written a poem every day —and testify to his dedication to the mastery of *form*. They also, of course, reveal important early themes and subject matter.

Included among Cummings' poetry workbooks and the college notebooks in which he wrote poems are many poetic exercises in traditional poetic forms, the ballad, the ballade, the heroic couplet, the heroic quatrain, the limerick, the rondeau, the rondel, the sonnet (Italian in form, more often than not), the Spenserian stanza, and the triplet. There are also exercises in alliterative verse, blank verse, elegaic stanzas, and free verse. There are also some poems in French. What are essentially study notes are sometimes included. Rhyme schemes and metrical patterns are worked out for many of the poems, and there are sometimes elaborate notes on possible combinations of rhyme schemes and metrical patterns. Some comments on musical notation suggest that Cummings may have been influenced by practicioners of musical scansion. The seriousness with which he regarded the craft of poetry is supported by such items as a listing of all the possible positions for the caesura in English translations of Latin dactylic hexameter. All in all, his workbooks show that Cummings was early dedicated to learning everything there was to know about the poetic possibilities of the English language.

Although it is usual to point out that Cummings' earliest published poems bear little resemblance to those for which he is now best known, the fact remains that they are a culmination of many years of disciplined writing and, if nothing else, demonstrate his competence as a versifier. In the best of them, there is already the originality and polish which marks the true poet. And occasionally there are flashes of that intensity of language and that freshness of voice which so often characterize his mature work. In "Summer Silence (Spenserian Stanza)," for instance, we read of "Thirst-stricken air, dumb-throated" and "the untranslated stars." That poem was first published in 1913. That same year appeared "Sunset" with its striving for freshness: "Great carnal mountains crouching in the cloud." But the highlight of that year's publication was the appearance of the lovely ballad "Of Nicolette," which is one of the earliest of his poems to be found in the later collections of his work.

The earliest traceable influences on form and style are those of the nineteenth-century poets generally. From them may stem the many early poems with ballad subjects and archaic language. "Of Nicolette" is typical of the best of these. It contains characteristic touches of a style that Cummings did not later abandon so much as transmute. That early style is important, partly because certain phrases—such as "the yellow wonder of her hair"—directly suggest the later Cummings. The particular style suggested here reached its culmination during the Harvard years in the justly famous "Ballad—All in Green went my love riding," which appeared in *The Harvard Monthly* for January, 1916. As other critics have suggested, the poem's success rests on its original combination of medieval ballad form and content with its variations from usual form and content. The rhyme scheme, in particular, has been varied. There is no apparent rhyme scheme; instead, rhyme is used as a device for emphasis. This particular element suggests the mature Cummings more than anything else about the poem, for the most consistent trademark of his mature poetry is his insistence on subordinating form to function.

Charles Norman has noted similarities between some lines from

Keats and some lines from Cummings. More important even than
the resemblances is a general legacy from Keats. There is evidence
in unpublished manuscripts to suggest that Cummings learned
much about poetic technique from his reading of Keats. For example, after reading "Lamia" in 1912, he copied into a notebook
lines from various sections of the poem. Then he made detailed
critical (sometimes syntactical) comments on many phrases and
lines in the various sections. Following that, there is a "List of
Impressions Which Various Vowels Give the Ear." Similar lists
occur in other manuscripts, and a grader's comment from 1915
shows that Cummings was encouraged in his regard for Keats's
poetic genius:

> Your reading of Keats of course shows through—watch his per-
> fect logical and grammatical joining of verse to verse without the
> inversions or use of 'who' or 'whose' of your last stanza. I can stand
> a good deal more of the same!

The influence of Shakespeare is a less direct one than that of
Keats, but it is in many ways more pervasive. Though Rossetti may
have been initially responsible for Cummings' fondness for the
sonnet as a poetic form, Shakespeare seems to have been the
dominant influence. That is particularly interesting in view of the
fact that he generally preferred the Italian or Petrarchan sonnet
to the English or Shakesperian sonnet. But he frequently combined the rhyme scheme of the Petrarchan sonnet with the characteristic Shakesperian placement of turn between the third quatrain
and the concluding couplet. That unusual placement of the turn also
suggests Milton, who also had an important indirect influence on
Cummings.

Other stylistic influences are worth noting. Cummings early
experimented with the Spenserian stanza; he apparently did not
find the form to his liking, for he soon stopped using it. That is
not surprising, for it does not lend itself to lyric purposes; it is
used primarily as a vehicle for narrative. He read Dante's sonnets, and some critics have felt that what appears to be an influence of the pre-Raphaelite school might as easily have been
picked up there. Throughout much of his career he wrote "songs
of praise" that are often Elizabethan in their tendency to be organized in sequence on a repetitive and parallelistic basis. That trait

seems to reflect the influence of such lyrics as Campion's "Cherry-Ripe" and Carew's "Ask Me No More," both of which are also songs of praise. All these influences were at work during the Harvard years. Fittingly, Cummings' first appearance in book form—his contributions to *Eight Harvard Poets*—occurred as a culmination of his literary endeavors and experiences at Harvard. *Eight Harvard Poets* included eight poems by Cummings, four of them sonnets:

> Thou in whose swordgreat story shine the deeds
> when thou hast taken thy last applause
> this is the garden: colours come and go
> it may not always be so; and i say

The first and third later appeared in *XLI Poems*, the second and fourth in the 1923 *Tulips and Chimneys*.

These sonnets are in some ways as good as some of Cummings' mature work; they are transitional in that they are still completely in the romantic vein which pervaded his early poetry. Of particular interest is the relationship between form and content in these sonnets. In form, all are perfectly conventional Italian sonnets, and the rhyme schemes are quite similar, each opening with an octave rhyming *abba abba* and concluding with a sestet involving rhymes *c*, *d*, and *e* in varying arrangements. Only the latter two sonnets have the turn occurring between the octave and the sestet, however. The first one has no real turn; the poem is in praise of Froissart, and the only real difference in kind of meaning occurring between the first and second parts of the poem is that he is mentioned by name only in the latter part. There is thus a move from the general to the particular, but the poem is most significantly a poem of praise. In the second poem there is a kind of movement to become very important in Cummings' later poems. The turn here occurs between lines thirteen and fourteen and preceeds a final, almost parenthetical comment, a kind of stage whisper that suggests the poet Heine as much as anyone else. It was a device that Cummings was to master completely. Here, as frequently, it introduces another point of view; in this case, it brings back to the poet *qua* poet:

> The lights have laughed their last; without, the street
> darkling awaiteth her whose feet have trod

the silly souls of men to golden dust:
she pauses on the lintel of defeat,
her heart breaks in a smile—and she is Lust . . . .

mine also, little painted poem of god
(I, 75)

Also of interest are the archaisms, frequent in the early poems.
Oddly, they are thick in the first two sonnets, those without the
conventional Italian turn, and absent from the latter two, which
are more traditional. Throughout Cummings' early poetry, archaisms are usually more frequent in strictly traditional forms; they
occur in both vocabulary and syntax. In the first sonnet here, there
are four *thou's*, a *didst*, and a *gavest*, and the genitive construc-
tion *of history her heroes*. In the second we find one *thou*, two
thy's, a *thee*, a *hast taken*, an *awaiteth*, and *without* in the sense
of "outside."

Already in evidence were certain typographical oddities for
which Cummings is well-known even by people who do not read
his poems. It is impossible to know at precisely what point in his
development unusual typography, capitalization, and punctuation
became important to Cummings. It is known, however, that there
was a problem about lower-case letters in connection with the
printing of *Eight Harvard Poets*. Norman has recorded that it
caused a "final flurry" in the book's publication, one that was re-
solved when the printer took it upon himself to capitalize all the
"i's." They were restored in *Tulips and Chimneys, XLI Poems,* and
& [AND]. Both Cummings and his admirers were (and still are)
likely to be asked why he made use of such apparent oddities. It is
always best to approach a literary figure, or any artist, on the
assumption that he wrote, or painted, or whatever, the way he did
for sound reasons; for that reason, it will be assumed—unless
examination proves otherwise—that Cummings wrote his poems
the way he wrote them for good reasons. It will further be assumed
that his unusual typography, capitalization, and punctuation
were used with good reason; one of his more interesting comments on the question was made in a letter to an unidentified
English correspondent many years later:

concerning the "small 'I' ": did it never strike you as significant
that,of all God'schildren,only English & American apotheosize their

55

egos by capitalizing a pronoun whose equivalent is in French "je" in German "ich", & in Italian "io"? (*Selected Letters*, p. 244)

Four other poems also appeared in *Eight Harvard Poets*:

> i will wade out
> Over silent waters
> your little voice
> Tumbling-hair

The first of these later appeared in *XLI Poems*, the third and fourth in the 1923 *Tulips and Chimneys*. The second one, entitled "Finis," has never been collected. These poems celebrate experience; the one not collected is less good than the others, primarily because of the rather maudlin touches and the conventional death imagery. More than the others it sounds like bad Tennyson and can serve as an example of the sort of expression of sentiment that Cummings soon outgrew, with its reference to "the gentle glory of the sunset" seen as "the last light's exhortation." These four, free of archaisms, are romantic and somewhat simplistic, and, with the exception of "Finis," they are delightful re-creations of spring experiences. In the first the speaker states his expectation of wading out until his "thighs are steeped in burning flowers" and he can set his teeth "in the silver of the moon" (I, 189). In the third there is a response to hearing on the telephone the voice of the beloved, "over time and tide and death" (I, 44). In the last one there is a picture of a flower picker, followed by "Another . . ./ also picking flowers" (I, 26).

The romantic vein characteristic of these early poems was much less in evidence after the publication of the manuscript *Tulips and Chimneys*. It is for rather special reasons the last full group of poems which belongs in a discussion of the early poetry. In order to understand the reasons for that, it is necessary to understand its publishing history. There are actually two published versions. The first, published in 1923, was an abridgement of the manuscript completed in 1922 that was not published in its entirety until 1937. That later edition carries on its title page the legend "ARCHETYPE EDITION OF THE ORIGINAL MS 1922". It contains poems that had appeared in & [AND] (1925), *XLI Poems* (1925), and *is 5* (1926), as well as those poems which had appeared in the 1923 *Tulips and Chimneys*. Obviously, all the poems of the original manuscript belong together for purposes of discussion, particularly since many of them were written when Cummings was at Harvard, some having appeared in slightly different form in the *Advocate* or the *Monthly*. The first *Tulips and Chimneys* contained 66 poems, the Archetype Edition, 150. Of the 84 poems apparently omitted from the original manuscript, 43 went to &, which also contained 36 new poems, and 41 went to make up the entire volume *XLI Poems*. Eight of the 43 which appeared in & also appeared in the original version of *is 5*. The poems of *Tulips and Chimneys* will be dealt with here as they appear in the original manuscript. Only the 36 new poems of & will be dealt with separately. *XLI Poems* will be mentioned only briefly, since all the poems in it are from the original manuscript. The reader should note that in all the real collections of Cummings' poems (the 1938 *Collected Poems* was inaccurately titled), the eight poems which appeared in both & and the original version of *is 5* were omitted from the *is 5* section and returned to &. Also, the two new poems which appeared in both & and *is 5* are retained only in the *is 5* section.

When the first publisher of *Tulips and Chimneys* reduced the manuscript from 150 poems to 66, he did so by cutting poems from each of the original divisions of the book, thus preserving the original organization. The two divisions "Tulips" and "Chimneys" give the volume its title, one that has been commented on by Friedman, who makes the observation that the division is more a stylistic one than a thematic one. He has pointed out that although one might think that "Tulips" refers to country poems and "Chimneys" to city poems, this does not seem to be the case. Rather, most of the "Tulips" are in free verse, representing "natural" or "organic" structures, while all the "Chimneys" are sonnets, thus representing "fixed" or "artificial" structures (the three long poems in the first section constitute the major exception; there are other minor ones, but the principle holds). The first edition omitted 40 of the original 89 poems under the "Tulips" heading, and 44 of the original 61 poems under the "Chimneys" heading. The nature of the omitted poems suggests that the reduction of the initial manuscript was a result of the publisher's unhappiness with the stress put upon sex and the demimonde in the original manuscript. Certainly, the published volume is different in overall tone from the original manuscript, and it may be assumed that tone did to a certain extent control critical and popular reception to the book. It also meant that there would be a heavier concentration of poems involving sex and the demimonde in the succeeding volumes; the first publisher, Thomas Seltzer, thus controlled the tone of subsequent publications to an extent. What appears to be a change in theme between the first and the next three books is partly the result of the initial pruning.

Shortened though it was, the appearance of the first edition of *Tulips and Chimneys* was important in a way no previous publication of Cummings had been. It was his first volume of poems to reach a general audience. At the time it appeared, he was, of course, already known to some as the author of *The Enormous Room*, and many of his readers were familiar with poems which had appeared in the pages of *The Dial*, *The Liberator*, *Broom*, *Secession*, *S-4-N*, and *Vanity Fair*. That is probably why his first volume of poems received a more sympathetic critical reception than might have been expected. Most of the serious attacks on his style were to come later.

The apparent eccentricities of style annoyed some readers from the start, however—even some readers otherwise disposed to like Cummings' poems. Harriet Monroe, for instance, the editor of *Poetry* magazine, praised the volume overall, but had reservations about what she called his "eccentric system of typography," as a result of which she tried "the experiment of printing him almost like anybody else, with the usual quantity of periods, commas, capital letters, and other generally accepted conventions of the printer's art" ("Flare and Blare," *Poetry*, XXIII, January, 1924, p. 212). The practice was neither emulated nor continued.

In view of the assumptions set out earlier, it will be useful at this point to examine certain facts about Cummings' poetry that are not always known or understood by the casual reader. First, Cummings is not significantly a "free verse" poet in the popular sense of that term. From first to last, he was a poet thoroughly in the tradition of English prosody; he experimented freely with given forms, but it will be seen that he molded traditional forms to new uses more often than he simply invented new ones. In this he resembles Swinburne as much as any other predecessor, and it is possible that he was heavily influenced by Swinburne's metrics.

Second, though there are no important "periods" in Cummings' life, as there are in the lives of poets like Eliot and Yeats, it is not true that there is no development in his poetry. He has been accused of such a lack of development, partly because he did not move from one clearly-defined "position" to another—politically or otherwise—during his lifetime. This has been somewhat unusual in twentieth-century America, though there are also the examples of Stevens and Frost. However, Cummings certainly matured and developed; the fact that his development cannot be charted in terms of "periods" does not belie that fact.

Further, Cummings was writing squarely in a tradition that began in America in the first half of the nineteenth century. Like Henry David Thoreau and Ralph Waldo Emerson, and later Walt Whitman, Cummings identified himself as an individual and poet similar to the model transcendentalist described in Emerson's essay, "The Transcendentalist." Like him, Cummings believed in the ultimate value of the egocentric individual and of love. He valued childhood. He scorned materialism and found society and institutions dangerous. Emerson's "spiritual principle" can be equated with Cummings' "love." Cummings was different from the early transcendentalists in one important way, though. He denied the flesh no more than did Whitman. Indeed, he sometimes appeared to have a naïve faith that if "spring omnipotent goddess" returns often enough and if people learn to "live suddenly without thinking," all will be well. That is, of course, a gross oversimplification of Cummings' philosophy, particularly as set forth in his mature poems, though it is true that when there is a choice to make, he is more likely than not to opt for the heart, not the head. It is important to keep in mind that Cummings was not often a victim of the "either/or" fallacy, that notion which says that things are good or bad, right or wrong, black or white. In many ways, in fact, his whole life was a protest against that fallacy.

In *Tulips and Chimneys* he set forth his basic concerns as a young poet. In later volumes, he was to refine his techniques of expression, modify his metaphysics, and move away from an early romanticism that threatened to dominate his poems, but he did not alter his basic concerns, which remained love and the individual. Before looking at the poems of *Tulips and Chimneys* which deal with these concerns, it will be useful to turn to a statement which explains a lesson learned by Cummings when he was a child being protected and sheltered by his family—except when he explored the nearby community of Somerville, shabby neighbor of respectable Cambridge:

> The more implacably a virtuous Cambridge drew me toward what might have been her bosom, the more sure I felt that soi-disant respectability comprised nearly everything I couldn't respect, and the more eagerly I explored sinful Somerville. But while a sinful Somerville certainly possessed a bosom (in fact, bosoms) she also possessed fists which hit below the belt and arms which threw snowballs containing small rocks. Little by little and bruise by teacup, my doubly disillusioned spirit made an awe-inspiring discovery; which (on more than several occasions) has prevented me from wholly misunderstanding socalled humanity: the discovery, namely, that all groups, gangs, and collectivities—no matter how apparently disparate—are fundamentally alike: and that what makes any world go round is not the trivial difference between a Somerville and a Cambridge, but the immeasurable difference between either of them and individuality. . . . Nor will anything ever persuade me that, by turning Somerville into Cambridge or Cambridge into Somerville or both into neither, anybody can make an even slightly better world. (*i:six nonlectures*, p. 31)

It is fair to say that the distance between total individuality and absolute collectivism is best measured in terms of a continuum. Neither extreme is ever realized in human life, but persons may be said to exist at various points along the continuum. The poems and experiences which Cummings celebrates most frequently and certainly most joyously occur to the left of center, politically speaking, while those "groups, gangs, and collectivities" he most disparages occur to the right of center. Throughout his poetic career, Cummings moved towards a position where politics and language correlate, but his early poems are not characterized by any such correlation. As Friedman has pointed out, Cummings' poems may be classified—according to vocabulary and what linguists call usage level—into three styles: the "formal" or "archaic," the "neutral," and the "mock" or "burlesque." Additionally, some poems contain a mixture of these, giving a fourth "style" or mode. The "neutral" style is more or less at the center, between the "'formal" or "archaic" at the extreme right, linguistically speaking, and the "mock" or "burlesque" at the extreme left. The neutral style is defined as

> a modified romantic style, which is romantic because of the quality and quantity of certain 'sweet," "warm," and "moist" words, such as *delicious* and *exquisite*, and modified because of the frequent intrusion of antipathetic or "plain," "hard," "cool," and "dry" words, such as *exact* and *stern*. . . . Varying to the right of this norm produces a purely serious, archaic, reverential, and formal style, while varying to the left creates a purely vulgar, violent, burlesque, and mock style; and, it is clear, each of these extremes has its special utility for glorifying and ridiculing, respectively. (*e. e. cummings: The Art of His Poetry*, p. 63)

As Friedman further points out, the "archaic" style, so frequent in Cummings' early works, becomes much less frequent in later works. And when it does appear, it is less "literary" and less derivative than it is in the early poems. The "burlesque" element becomes correspondingly more important in Cummings' later works.

The poems in *Tulips and Chimneys*, though formally divided into but two long divisions, actually fall into three categories. Three poems in the "Tulips" section—"Epithalamion," "Of Nicolette," and "Puella Mea"—are so different from other poems in the section as to constitute a separate section. They are all fairly conventional poems, and they are marked by archaisms of language and syntax. The first consists of twenty-one eight-line pentameter stanzas; the second consists of four eight-line pentameter stanzas; and the third consists of seven and a half pages of irregular-rhyming tetrameter lines. Couplets dominate in "Puella Mea," but there are also passages which give the appearance of being practice runs for the sestet sections of Petrarchan sonnets. "Puella Mea" is certainly the most interesting of these three long poems, and it contains a higher proportion of lines which suggest the mature Cummings. Later poems reiterate the sentiment expressed in such a couplet as this:

> If she a little turn her head
> i know that i am wholly dead:
> (I, 17)

The poem is, however, derivative, and much of it reads as an exercise in literary one-upmanship:

61

(Whose rideth in the tale
of Chaucer knoweth many a pair
of companions blithe and fair;
who to walk with Master Gower
in Confessio doth prefer
shall not lack for beauty there,
nor he that will amaying go
with my lord Boccaccio—
whoso knocketh at the door
of Marie and of Maleore
findeth of ladies goodly store
whose beauty did in nothing err.
(I, 20–21)

The other poems in the "Tulips" section constitute a small collection of poems, more often than not in a kind of free verse, whose subject matter ranges from love to war. Formally, there are eight sub-divisions. The first, called "Songs," is placed between "Of Nicolette" and "Puella Mea"; the poems in it are like the three longer poems in that they are conventional in form (only one is in free verse) and derivative in subject matter and theme. The remaining sections are titled as follows: Chansons Innocentes, Orientale, Amores, La Guerre, Impressions, Portraits, and Post Impressions. Among these poems are some of the best-loved of Cummings' poems. We shall examine them in terms of the four basic styles that seem most important when the poetry is approached in terms of intent and statement: one is romantic; another is satiric, usually accompanied by a strong sense of indignation; a third, most often found in portrait poems, lies somewhere between romance and satire—its tone is one of appreciation, implying neither approval nor indignation; the fourth style, more difficult to label, results in a "tricky" poem, sometimes with epigrammatic and sometimes with haiku effect.

There are two kinds of romantic poems. The earlier ones in this style, including many of those in *Tulips and Chimneys*, tend to be filled with archaisms, with such forms as *thee* and *thou* and *dost* being very frequent. A good example of an early romantic poem is the one which appeared as Portrait XXI. It begins with an invocation to "spring omnipotent goddess" which within a few

lines becomes an acknowledgement of the fact that "spring slat-
tern of seasons" has "dirty legs and a muddy petticoat" and has
been known to sing in a "whiskey-voice." The poem concludes
with a celebration of sensation; while it is by no means reminiscent of Shelley in tone, it is thematically close to that poet's
recognition of the cyclical nature of this world:

> for thou comest and your hands
> are the snow
> and thy fingers are the rain,
> and i hear
> the screech of dissonant
> flowers, and most of all
> i hear your stepping
>
> > freakish feet
> > feet incorrigible
>
> ragging the world,
> (I, 61)

The concluding comma suggests continuity and on-goingness; it
is an early instance of the way in which Cummings could use conventional punctuation marks in unconventional ways to achieve
the economy and compression most characteristic of his best
poetry.

An early example of a romantic poem which is less filled with
archaisms—and which suggests the more mature romantic poems
—is the justly famous Chansons Innocentes I which describes the
arrival in early Spring of the "little lame balloonman" who, when
he whistles, summons the neighbourhood children at play in a
world that is "puddle-wonderful." The poem is characterized by
a freshness and sensitivity to the essentially amoral character of
the universe; the innocence of childhood play is only intensified
by the poet's recognition that the old balloonman introduces into
the scene a potentially satyric note:

> it's
> spring
> and
> > the
> > > goat-footed
> > balloonMan   whistles

63

far
and
wee
(I, 24)

The language of the poem is suggestive of some poems which seem designed to make their special appeal to children. One is a brief catalogue of "little ghost-things"; it makes use of onomatopoeia and repetition to establish its appeal. Some lines of Chansons Innocentes II illustrate the techniques used:

little hoppy happy
toad in tweeds
tweeds
little itchy mousies

with scuttling
eyes   rustle and run   and
hidehidehide
whisk
(I, 25)

The early poems of satire are much less filled with indignation than the later ones. In *Tulips and Chimneys*, the poems of satire occur in two sections, "La Guerre" and the "SONNETS REALITIES" of Chimneys. Most striking in the Tulips section is one in which the poet introduces an attitude that is to be of paramount importance in all his works, an awareness of the incredible distance between mankind, on the one hand, and individual man, on the other. This particular poem is devoted solely to an examination of the abstract concept "mankind." It is important that the poem not be read as a condemnation of man the individual:

Humanity i love you
because you would rather black the boots of
success than enquire whose soul dangles from his
watch-chain which would be embarrassing for both

parties and because you
unflinchingly applaud all
songs containing the words country home and
mother when sung at the old howard

Humanity i love you because
when you're hard up you pawn your

64

intelligence to buy a drink and when
you're flush pride keeps

you from the pawn shop and
because you are continually committing
nuisances but more
especially in your own house

Humanity i love you because you
are perpetually putting the secret of
life in your pants and forgetting
it's there and sitting down

on it
and because you are
forever making poems in the lap
of death Humanity

i hate you
(I, 204)

The portrait poems in this volume fall into two categories, those describing the demimonde and those describing more conventionally acceptable subjects. The former describe a world peopled by whores, bums, and unfortunate children; it is inhabited by Marj and Lil, and it tells of strong men whose hands curl around beers, of the deaths of old men, about sailors shuffling in the night, and about waddling madams and their customers. Occasionally, one of the poems is cast in the form of a dramatic monologue; one such example is Portrait XXVIII, beginning "raise the shade/ will youse dearie?" (I, 109). Two features of this poem deserve special attention; it is one of the earliest poems in which it is clear that the poet is assuming a voice not his own, and it is one of the earliest poems in which the poet portrays his speaker partly through the use of dialect. The poem actually makes use of both pronunciation spelling—as in *youse* and *yer*—and what should be called "eye-dialect," that is, the use of quasi-phonetic spelling intended primarily to suggest a broadly comic effect, not to convey a character's speech as carefully as possible. The spelling of *awl* (for *all*) in this poem is an example of eye-dialect.

Cummings' use of dialect is confined for the most part to what Friedman has called "New Yorkese vulgarisms"—they are generally representative of the speech of uneducated New Yorkers, with a distinctive dialect, approximately that of Brooklyn. In his renderings of the dialect pattern, Cummings often exaggerates, so that the effect is usually at least partly that of caricature. Among those represented thus are prostitutes—as above—and later politicians, Jews, Bowery bums, fundamentalist preachers, and super-patriots.

Cummings' use of dialect is quite different from the techniques used in the "tricky" poems. Though these sometimes have epigrammatic or haiku effect, they may also result in what Friedman has called typographs. Deservedly, one of the best-known in *Tulips and Chimneys* is this favorite:

```
Buffalo Bill's
defunct
        who used to
        ride a watersmooth-silver
                              stallion
and break onetwothreefourfive pigeonsjustlikethat
                                            Jesus
        he was a handsome man
                      and what i want to know is
        how do you like your blueeyed boy
        Mister Death
        (I, 60)
```

That is by no means the whole bag of tricks, so far as the typographs are concerned. The devices used here—irregular spacing of lines, the running together of words to indicate tempo and simultaneity, the spacing-out of words to indicate separation—are but the beginning of Cummings' typographical style. But a direction has been pointed.

When we turn to "Chimneys," we discover that the subdivisions within that section of the book also correspond to subject matter, and, to some extent, to style, also. The first, SONNETS-REALITIES, deals primarily with physical love and the demimonde; the second, SONNETS-UNREALITIES, deals with nature and idealized romantic love; the third, SONNETS-ACTUALITIES, contains poems which more nearly resemble portrait poems than anything else. In form, most of Cummings' sonnets are Petrarchan, rather than Shakesperian. It is difficult to classify them exactly, partly because of the liberties he took with the form. Further, he occasionally combined elements of one type with elements of another type. Occasionally, he placed the turn so near the end of the poem that it practically occurs outside the poem proper. A useful way of examining the sonnets, then, is not in terms of their internal structure, but in terms of the various styles which have already been mentioned.

One of the most successful, if derivative, of Cummings' romantic sonnets is one which reminds many readers of Edna St. Vincent Millay. The projected sense of distance dwelt upon by the speaker suggests the deliberate melancholy often indulged in by late nineteenth-century poets, and the bittersweet, highly oxymoronic indulgence of mood heightens that suggestion. Additionally, the "objective correlative" in the closing lines suggests the kinds of images favored by those poets. Cummings' poem begins with the speaker's bemused recognition that his mistress may not always love him, and it concludes with his imagined response to a situation in which she loves another:

> if this should be, i say if this should be—
> you of my heart, send me a little word;
> that i may go unto him, and take his hands,
> saying, Accept all happiness from me.
> Then shall i turn my face, and hear one bird
> sing terribly afar in the lost lands.
> (I, 76)

This poem contains one interesting weakness that often mars the early poems—that is the wordiness of the first line quoted. As Cummings matured, he developed an economy of expression that was one of his greatest virtues as a poet.

In a celebration of bohemian existence which skirts satire without ever quite approaching it, the poet gently mocks the form:

> my sonnet is A light goes on in
> the toiletwindow, that's straightacross from
> my window, night air bothered with a rustling din
>
> sort of sublimated tom-tom
> which quite outdoes the mandolin—
> man's tiny racket.
> (I, 171)

67

Many of the sonnets in *Tulips and Chimneys* are portrait poems explicitly concerned with sex; a high proportion of them deal with sex as it is initiated or practiced at houses of prostitution. One describes a customer's arrival at Dick Mid's Place, where "the madam was a bulb stuck in the door," and where

> —If they knew you at Dick Mid's
> the three twinkling chins began to traipse
> into the cheeks "eet smeestaire steevunsun
> kum een, dare ease Bet, an Leelee, an dee beeg wun"
> her handless wrists did gooey severe shapes.
> (I, 73)

By very definition, a sonnet cannot be a typograph, in the sense in which the word is being used of Cummings' poems. For the same reason, not all the sonnets fall neatly into the division noted earlier in Cummings' style. One stylistic device worth noting, used particularly in rather free-wheeling sonnet structures, is the use of a final qualifying statement to modify the tone of what has preceded it. As suggested earlier, the use of this device has the effect of putting the turn in the poem but a few words from the end of it. It is used most often to transform what appears at first to be a romantic poem into a satiric poem, sometimes gently, sometimes more stridently. Here is one example of the use of the device:

> yours is the music for no instrument
> yours the preposterous colour unbeheld
>
> —mine the unbought contemptuous intent
> till this our flesh merely shall be excelled
> by speaking flower
>   (if i have made songs
>
> it does not greatly matter to the sun,
> nor will rain care
>   cautiously who prolongs
> unserious twilight) shadows have begun
>
> the hair's worm huge, ecstatic, rathe . . . .
>
> yours are the poems i do not write.

In this at least we have got a bulge on death,
silence, and the keenly musical light

of sudden nothing . . . . la bocca mia "he
kissed wholly trembling"
                                    or so thought the lady
(I, 84)

3

The Poetry

Since the unconventional aspects of Cummings' poetry are sometimes concentrated on to the exclusion of other features, it might be well to begin with a brief examination of some misunderstandings of these elements. Observations about them are often inaccurate and lead to serious misreadings of the poems. Though it should, for instance, go without saying that the poems of Cummings, like those of all true poets, are written primarily for the ear, not the eye, the fact of the matter is that many are disposed to take Cummings at his most atypical and single out the exceptions for the rule. His "eye-poems" constitute a negligible percentage of his total body of poems; at their worst they are curiosities—and any poet is entitled to a curiosity or two. At their best the poems belong in that respectable tradition of poems—going back at least to Alexandria—which make at least part of their appeal to the eye, including poems by poets like Guillaume Apollinaire, F. T. Marinetta, Mina Loy and possibly also George Herbert, Lewis Carroll, and Dylan Thomas.

To be sure, Cummings' most famous "eye-poem," about the grasshopper, is no *carmen figuratum*; place it beside Herbert's "Easter Wings" or the "long and sad tail of the Mouse" in *Alice in Wonderland* or Thomas's "Vision and Prayer" and the differences are striking. All these poems, however, appeal in part to the eye. The "grasshopper" poem is often cited as a good example of an "unreadable" Cummings poem – i.e., a poem which makes its *total* appeal to the eye. In truth, of course, only certain parts of the poem are unreadable, that is unpronounceable. A close examination will reveal which parts can be pronounced and which parts cannot be:

70

r-p-o-p-h-e-s-s-a-g-r
            who
a)s w(e loo)k
upnowgath
            PPEGORHRASS
                        eringint(o-
aThe):l
      eA
        !p:
S   a
            (r
   rIvInG   .gRrEaPsPhOs)
                                    to
rea(be)rran(com)gi(e)ngly
,grasshopper;
(I, 396)

Obviously, the poet has set out to show us in language what a
grasshopper looks like as he jumps. He first gathers himself up,
transforming himself into a creature ready to jump. Then he leaps.
At the moment he lands, he is arranged still differently from the
way he looked when he gathered himself up to leap. So he must re-
arrange himself to become once more a grasshopper in stasis. It
is totally appropriate that the "word" *grasshopper* appears in its
conventional form only in the last line of the poem.

The poet has shown us on the printed page—in "words" (some
of which are unconventional, and some of which are unpronounceable, but all of which are recognizable)—the process involved in
a grasshopper's leap. More, he has pictured the actual leap. He has
done this in a spirit of play that allows him to include humor.
The poem is a witty one, because the humor in it allows us a
glimpse not only of the grasshopper, whose essence is defined by
his action, but also of the poet, sitting to one side and forcing the
reader to view the action from his point of view.

It is clear that Cummings thinks of himself as a "maker" from
his statement, "If a poet is anybody, he is somebody to whom
things made matter very little—somebody who is obsessed by
Making" ("Foreword" to *is 5*, I, 223). The implication is clear that
"making" is process, is life, while "made" is stasis, is death.

Other poems of Cummings make an important appeal to the
eye. The most interesting treatment of these poems has been that

of Norman Friedman, who has pointed out that they have central significance for Cummings' transcendentalism. He has said that these "typographs" are neither jokes nor trivia; rather, they are a means by which nature's dynamic process may be glimpsed, and the glimpse be passed on to the reader, who may thereby achieve transcendental vision.

Cummings himself has commented on the subject of these poems. Some, he says, are not meant to be read aloud; they are meant to be seen and not heard. Many of the typographs that cannot be read aloud do, nevertheless, make a large part of their appeal to the ear. Their unique structures on the page certainly add dimensions to their existence, but some are quite pronounceable. In fact, only two other poems of the *Complete Poems* are significantly unpronounceable. They are poems 38 and 46 of *No Thanks* (I, 421 and 429). So it is apparent that what has been regarded as a problem—or at least a peculiarity—is in reality a minor exception, greatly distorted and magnified.

Some poems, of course, must be read aloud with an ordering of sounds slightly different from that which appears on the page. A good example of such a poem is the rather stark and apparently generally startling poem which opened the volume *95 Poems* (1958):

l(a

le
af
fa

ll

s)
one
l

iness
(II, 673)

That we would normally read this aloud as "a leaf falls: loneliness" is no evidence that there is anything defective about the poem. The significance of the vocal re-ordering lies only in the fact that the eye is faster than the ear and much faster than the organs of articulation. And neither is it evidence that "a leaf falls:

loneliness" would have been "just as good"—the one *is* a poem, the other *attempts* to recapitulate in the logic of prose what the poem *is*. Much would be lost if the poem were presented in any other way. The poem is able to take advantage of the fact that the letter *l* is, in print, identical with the cardinal numeral *1*. Thus, the placement of the letter *l* directly under the line reading "one" allows for visual re-enforcement of the notion that being one is being alone. Poems like this one are among the earliest examples of concrete poetry.

Just as Cummings' poems are directed primarily to the ear, so are the various devices by means of which he gets his poems arranged on the page largely directed to the oral readings of the poems. It is important to look at these devices closely, both because they have annoyed and puzzled some readers, and because they are important and interesting in their own right. The easiest way to approach them is to hear them in action; that can be done by listening to recordings of Cummings reading his poems. It is highly instructive to follow the text of a given poem while listening to the poet's reading of it. Parentheses, commas, spaced-out words, bunched-up words—all these devices emerge as stage directions of a sort. The simplest devices are those of disjunction and displacement. These devices are sometimes combined; an element of a word may appear parenthetically within another word. This is one way of suggesting a simultaneity of action or experience which cannot be expressed by ordinary syntax. Inherent in the English language is a false chronology which announces that one thing always follows another thing. A language built on a subject-verb-object rendering of experience must be wrenched a bit if one is to portray experience more nearly as it is. Friedman has said that Cummings wrote English as if it were an inflected language, like Latin or German. Certainly, it is true that the kind of analysis needed to read poems which begin like this one more nearly resembles the process of unscrambling word order in a German sentence than in the usual English sentence:

> nonsum blob a
> cold to
> skylessness
> sticking fire
> (II, 541)

73

Clearly, this poem will require a certain amount of unscrambling. It also requires a recognition that Cummings' use of words is such that he gets greater mileage from even such simple words as "a" and "and" and "the" than the writer of an ordinary English sentence is likely to. Word coinages are another trademark of Cummings. In this poem one notes "nonsun," "skylessness," and "unearth" (not quoted). These are typical coinages, for Cummings most often created new words by the use of inflectional or derivational affixes. In this respect, he was typical of his period, for other writers—Dos Passos and Faulkner certainly come to mind—used affixes to create new words. What is unusual is that Cummings did this in poetry, while others used the technique mostly in prose writings.

More important than the specific devices used by Cummings is the use to which he puts the devices. That is a complex matter; irregular spacing, either of whole words or parts of words, for instance, allows both amplification and retardation. Further, spacing of key words allows puns which would otherwise be impossible. Some devices, such as the use of lowercase letters at the beginnings of lines and for the first person personal pronoun, allow a kind of distortion that often re-enforces that of the syntax. Friedman has suggested that both seem to spring from a conviction that it is necessary to transform the word in order to transform the world. All these devices have the effect of jarring the reader, of forcing him to examine experience with fresh eyes.

Not all the devices are used with the same frequency throughout Cummings' career as a poet. The earliest poetry is characterized by a great deal of synaesthesia, personification, metaphor, and simile. It is much more conventional than the later poetry, which relies increasingly on symbol, allegory, paradox, word-coinage, typographical spacing, and oxymoron. For a more detailed treatment of Cummings' use of these devices and of the ways in which they give evidence of Cummings' growth, see Friedman's *The Art of His Poetry*.

The subject matter of Cummings' poems may be approached in terms of the stylistic breakdown set forth in the preceding chapter. Some initial generalizations will be useful. The romantic poems, predictably, have for their subjects such things as love,

nature, Spring, birds, flowers, kisses, sunsets, youth, rain, stars—
mostly the little and potentially intimate natural occurrences.
The satiric poems deal with quite different kinds of subjects; love
may appear, but it will do so only in terms of its physical manifestation, and most often on city streets where the actors will be
whores and pimps and their customers or potential customers.
This is not to suggest that Cummings was opposed to sex—quite
the contrary!—but rather to suggest that once sex becomes exclusively a commercial venture, it is subject to the same ridicule
and contempt as any form of commercial exploitation—and Cummings' opinion of salesmen can readily be deduced from the poem
beginning "a salesman is an it that stinks Excuse" (II, 549). The
range of Cummings' satiric subjects also includes capitalism, with
particular attention to American advertising; war; Communism;
western technology, generally; politics and politicians; do-gooders
of various sorts; big shots of any kind; bureaucrats and bureaucracy; -ism's generally—and, finally, "mostpeople."

A word of caution is in order with regard to that last item;
because of his expressed disdain for "mostpeople," Cummings has
sometimes been accused of being a snob. It is important to remember that Cummings' first discussion of the concept "mostpeople,"
which occurred in the "Introduction" to *Collected Poems* (1938),
was by way of opposing "you and I," who are "human beings" to
"mostpeople," who are "snobs." Cummings' appeal to his reader
makes it clear that human beings cannot be snobs:

> Take the matter of being born. What does being born mean to
> mostpeople? Catastrophe unmitigated. Socialrevolution. The cul-
> tured aristocrat yanked out of his hyperexclusively ultravoluptuous
> superpalazzo, and dumped into an incredibly vulgar detentioncamp
> swarming with every conceivable species of undesirable organism.
> Mostpeople fancy a guaranteed birthproof safetysuit of non-
> destructible selflessness. If mostpeople were to be born twice they'd
> improbably call it dying—
> you and I are not snobs. We can never be born enough. We are
> human beings; for whom birth is a supremely welcome mystery, the
> mystery of growing: the mystery which happens only and when-
> ever we are faithful to ourselves. You and I wear the dangerous
> looseness of doom and find it becoming. Life, for eternal us, is now;

75

and now is much too busy being a little more than everything to seem anything, catastrophic included. (II, 461)

If one compares Cummings' comments on "mostpeople" with his often tender portraits of the rather unlovely specimens of humanity he deals with in every volume of poems, he must, to be fair, admit that Cummings seems to be an individual who hates humanity—i.e., the abstract notion of mankind, the mass-i-ness of mass-men—because he loves individual men. Some poets are able to love humanity because they hate men. Certainly, it is important to distinguish between the mass-i-ness of mass-men and men themselves. That Cummings was able to do so is shown in this poem:

> a man who had fallen among thieves
> lay by the roadside on his back
> dressed in fifteethrate ideas
> wearing a round jeer for a hat
>
> fate per a somewhat more than less
> emancipated evening
> had in return for consciousness
> endowed him with a changeless grin
>
> whereon a dozen staunch and leal
> citizens did graze at pause
> then fired by hypercivic zeal
> sought newer pastures or because
>
> swaddled with a frozen brook
> of pinkest vomit out of eyes
> which nobody noticed he looked
> as if he did not care to rise
>
> one hand did nothing on the vest
> its wideflung friend clenched weakly dirt
> while the mute trouserfly confessed
> a button solemnly inert.
>
> Brushing from whom the stiffened puke
> i put him all into my arms
> and staggered banged with terror through
> a million billion trillion stars
> (I, 258)

76

The subjects of the portrait poems are, of course, individuals, many of them as unlovely as the "man who had fallen among thieves." For many of them Cummings the poet has appreciation, his tone implying neither approval nor indignation. The portrait poems also include conventionally acceptable subjects; in fact, characters from the demimonde diminish in later volumes. Finally, the subjects of the typographs, the "tricky" poems, sometimes with epigrammatic and sometimes with haiku effect, tend to be similar to those of the romantic poems. They often involve the celebration of sensation; since they are organic structures which often show process, Becoming as opposed to Being, they tend to depict, rather than delimit. Thus, they are seldom characterized by attitudinal strictures.

Cummings' metrics have not yet been adequately dealt with; indeed, a thorough study of that subject will have to wait until principles of versification in English are better understood than they presently are. Until such time as a complete study of Cummings' metrics can be done, much will be left unsaid about his poetry, for as Ezra Pound noted some years ago, in an unpublished review of *Collected Poems*, a serious discussion of Cummings will be found in the end to be largely criticism of the technique of meter, a matter of versification. There has been *some* serious study of Cummings' metrics, particularly by Norman Friedman, and the present study is indebted to what has already been done.

The "devices" discussed above are elements of Cummings' order in his poems, and, as such, they play an important role in the shaping of the poems. Of greater importance, though, is poetic meter strictly defined: a more or less regular linguistic rhythm, resulting from the heightened, organized, and regulated natural rhythmical movements of colloquial speech—so that pattern emerges from the relative phonetic haphazardness of ordinary utterance—which is the most fundamental technique of order available to the poet. Some other poetic techniques of order—rhyme, line division, stanzaic form, and over-all structure—are in a sense projections and magnifications of the kind of formal repetition which is meter. One may, with Paul Fussell, want to consider these other techniques to be "meter writ large."

Cummings' metrics are complex; they range from what have

been called the "spatial cadences" of his typographs and some other poems to a fairly stable system of accentual-syllabism, the staple system for poetry in Modern English. Somewhere between these extremes of experiment and the traditional metrical patterns are occasional departures from those patterns, sometimes even to the point of complete departure from any prosodic system. It is interesting to note the extent to which Cummings' metrics suggest the range of metrical possibilities explored by American poets. Most of the "temporary prosodic mutations" which have taken place in this century have been associated with the United States, rather than with Britain; such poets as Cummings and Marianne Moore have been the most inventive and also most metrically learned of the experimenters. Additionally, Cummings has written some of the smoothest and stablest of lyrics using traditional metrical patterns. Critics familiar only or primarily with his typographs and other experimental forms are apt to overlook Cummings' strength as a poet writing in the tradition of English verse. The fact is that he is one of the rare poets who can, because he is so metrically learned and inventive, strengthen the traditional patterns of metrics by ringing changes on them.

Closely associated with meter, strictly speaking, in Cummings' poems, are the other poetic techniques of order mentioned above, particularly that of stanza form, which really incorporates the techniques of rhyme and line division and which, together with meter, produces the overall structure of any given poem. All poems, of course, employ one of two kinds of basic organization, stichic or strophic; Cummings employs both types of organization, the former most often in his typographs, the latter both in traditional forms, such as the sonnet, and in nonce forms of his own creation. If his poems are classified strictly on the basis of meter and stanza form, it appears that Cummings' metrical accomplishment can be most basically examined in terms of a scale on which there are basically five types of poems. Going from left to right, from least traditional to most traditional, these are typographs, nonce forms combining traditional metrical features with non-traditional features, nonce forms using traditional metrical patterns, fixed forms incorporating non-traditional metrical features, and fixed forms using only traditional metrical patterns.

The complete texts of two typographs have already been given, those of the grasshopper poem and "a leaf falls: loneliness." The former, presented as an example of an "eye-poem," is unusual in that it is one of the few poems by Cummings which cannot be read aloud; the latter, presented as an example of a poem which must be read aloud with an ordering of sounds slightly different from that which appears on the page, is, while not so unusual, one of a rather small number of poems falling into the same category. Some of the poems in that category require a vocal re-ordering which is more orderly and systematic than the one given above. In the following poem, for instance, the word "slowliest" must vocally precede or follow the rest of the poem. Its arrangement on the page, however, suggests that its function is continuing modification. Because of the weather, everything seems to be happening in slow motion, as it were:

> un
> der fog
> 's
> touch

> slo

> ings
> fin
> gering
> s

> wli

> whichs
> turn
> in
> to whos

> est

> people
> be
> come
> un
> (II, 463)

This poem is important and interesting for a number of reasons. First, there is the dual vocal track on which it operates; the reading of "slowliest" really *ought* to parallel the reading of what may be called the body of the poem. That it cannot conveniently do so ordinarily does not detract from the excellence of the poem; it does, however, say something about the relationship between art and life. Things are possible in the one that are not possible in the other.

It is also a good example of a poem dependent on Cummings' special poetic vocabulary, what Friedman has called his conceptual vocabulary. It is part of his working solution to the problem of the inherent tendency of language to abstraction; by making nouns out of verbs, adverbs, adjectives, and so on—here, pronouns —he managed to suggest motion and structure where the conventional language would have preserved only stasis and function. The grammatical shifts result in metaphors of a sort and surround the kernel meaning of each word thus shifted with many potential connotations. In this particular poem, the key words are "whichs" as opposed to "whos" and "people" as opposed to "un." In his later use of this conceptual vocabulary, Cummings consistently used the word "which" to refer to a depersonalized human being, a nonperson; similarly, "who" always means an individual, a human being. Krushchev, for instance, is once described as "a which that walks like a who" (II, 711). Cummings' use of these perfectly ordinary words in rather special ways results in an enormous richness of connotation for the reader who is aware of the special uses to which Cummings has put them.

And, finally, the subject matter of the poem is interesting. Brief as the poem is, it tells a story, complete with beginning, middle, and end. In the brief narrative, the poet pictures someone in a fog heavy enough that it appears to "touch" and "finger" the body of the person. Other people approach and pass him. Coming towards him they resemble *things* until they are quite close, at which point "whichs" turn into "whos." Receding, they quickly become unrecognizable as human beings: "people become un." The message is simple enough on the face of it. Implicit in the poem, however, is the strong suggestion that closeness is part of being human and that distance may disguise—or even change—one's humanity. In the poem that suggestion is couched in physical

80

terms, but it would be the rare reader who would not immediately translate the concept into metaphysical terms. The fog, a "natural" phenomenon, is neutral in this respect. Both actions—that of "whichs" becoming "whos" and that of "people" becoming "un"— take place under fog's "touchings" and "fingerings." This fact suggests another metaphysical truth, namely that only human beings have both positive and negative potential, that is, the power for good or evil.

Another kind of typograph requiring either vocal re-ordering or the use of hesitation as a poetic element is that in which the re-ordering—or the hesitation—is necessitated by the use of a special kind of parenthesis, a technique Cummings used well and frequently. This technique is a common one in modern literature; it has been used by novelists interested in reporting as accurately as possible the highly fluid and unstable nature of thought and feeling, most notably Joyce and Faulkner. Their use of parenthesis is often characterized by a lack of formal punctuation. Cummings' use of it is almost always characterized by formal, if sometimes unconventional punctuation. In the following poem, he does use the conventional curved marks indicating parenthesis:

```
                              i will be
          M o ving in the Street of her

          bodyfee l inga ro undMe the traffic of
          lovely;muscles-sinke x p i r i n   g S
                uddenl
          Y              totouch
                         the curvedship of
                                        Her-
          . . . .kIss      her: hands
                          will play on,mE as
          dea d tunes OR s-cra p-y leaVes flut te rin g
          from Hideous trees or

             Maybe Mandolins
                        l oo k-
             pigeons fly ingand

          whee(: are,SpRiN,k,LiNg an in-stant with sunLight
          t h e n)l-
```

81

ing all go BlacK wh-eel-ing

oh
   ver
      m
         mYveRylitTle
street
where
you will come,
        at twi li ght

s(oon & there's
  a   m oo
)n.
   (I, 122)

This poem is noteworthy as an example of Cummings' tendency to portray sexual experience in terms of urban or technological imagery. It calls to mind the better-known "she being Brand" (I, 248), a parody of man's very twentieth-century concern with the automobile; ostensibly about breaking in a new car, it is obviously about making love to a virgin.

His nonce forms—those invented for a single poetic occasion—make up something over half of Cummings' published poems, depending upon whether one includes among them the typographs, with which the reader is least likely to be happy with the word "forms"; therefore, the term "nonce forms" has been reserved for those poems in which meter, strictly defined, is present, and about which the term "stanza form" has some real meaning. Some of these poems make use of metrical features recognizable as traditional ones; others do not. Many of these, of course, could be called free verse. But when that term is made—as it often is today—to describe the poetic accomplishments of poets as diverse as Walt Whitman, Amy Lowell, T. S. Eliot, and even the authors of the Old Testament *Psalms* and *Song of Solomon*, as well as the antics of Allen Ginsberg, then it does seem that some more meaningful way of describing contemporary poetic achievement is in order. Hence the present classification—in terms of which, the next category to be discussed, the nonce forms which combine traditional metrical features with non-traditional features, is the one whose members most deserve to be called free verse.

The earliest examples of this category were seen in the *Tulips and Chimneys* manuscript, after which they quickly became fewer in number. Some are to be found in *is 5* (1926); the one below illustrates a mild kind of *joie de vivre* in which Cummings sometimes exulted. Note its simple dependence on rhymes reminiscent of popular songs, on repetition of key words, and on the for once non-exaggerated use of New York vulgarisms:

> Jimmie's got a goil
> > > goil
> > > > goil,
> > > > > Jimmie
>
> 's got a goil and
> she coitnly can shimmie
>
> when you see her shake
> > > shake
> > > > shake,
> > > > > when
>
> you see her shake a
> shimmie how you wish that you was Jimmie.
>
> Oh for such a gurl
> > > gurl
> > > > gurl,
> > > > > oh
>
> for such a gurl to
> be a fellow's twistandtwirl
>
> talk about your Sal-
> > > Sal-
> > > > Sal-,
> > > > > talk
>
> about your Salo
> -mes but gimmie Jimmie's gal.
> (I, 235)

In the same volume are found some satires in the same style, most of which attack American institutions and pompousness. One short one, a four-liner with an unusual (for Cummings) *aabb* rhyme scheme, makes use of dialect for a rather serious comment on a sacred institution:

now dis "daughter" uv eve(who aint precisely slim)sim

ply don't know duh meanin uv duh woid sin in
not disagreeable contras tuh dat not exacly fat

"father"(adjustin his robe)who now puts on his flat hat
(I, 240)

Those who think of Cummings as the poet of lowercase letters, scrambled words, and largely unpronounceable poems are always surprised to learn how many and what excellent poems he wrote using traditional metrical features. Really, the most interesting— and often the most successful—of his poems are those which are nonce forms using traditional metrical patterns. They become most important after *is 5*, which begins a turning point in Cummings' poetic development. As Norman Friedman has pointed out, it is by that volume becoming apparent that in general Cummings reserves metrical stanzas for his more "serious" poems, while he uses experiments for various kinds of free verse embodiments of satire, comedy, and description. The "serious" poems are not all solemn. They are serious in that they embody a more complex view of the universe—and man's place in it—than is possible in the other poems. It is in these that Cummings' transcendent vision is more thoroughly revealed and in which love is described in terms of a transcendental metaphor. Satire is also included; one early example is a satiric poem on the subject of war. First published in *W [ViVa]* (1931), it involves the story of Olaf, a conscientious objector modeled on someone Cummings had met at Camp Devens. In the poem Olaf is first hazed, then tortured, and finally put to death because he does not believe in war. The poem consists of forty-two lines, the pattern for each of which is an eight-syllable, four-stress line, with occasional three-stress lines for variation. The basic foot is the iamb; the basic metrical pattern, iambic tetrameter, is one traditionally used for satiric purposes. While no overall rhyme scheme divides the poem into regular stanzas, there is a discernible impulse toward order; lines are interlocked, and motifs are picked up by the rhyme, even though it is not regular. In that respect it is similar to the three long poems of *Tulips and Chimneys*, particularly "Puella Mea." From its opening lines—"i sing of Olaf glad and big/whose warmest heart

84

recoiled at war:"—to its inevitable conclusion, it is a poem
dominated by suggestions of scatalogy and emphasis upon the dis-
crepancies of which institutional life is always compounded. Olaf
speaks twice, once to announce that he "will not kiss your f.ing
flag," once to re-affirm "there is some s. I will not eat." Olaf ends
in a dungeon; the poem concludes on this note:

> Christ(of His mercy infinite)
> i pray to see; and Olaf, too
>
> preponderatingly because
> unless statistics lie he was
> more brave than me:more blond than you.
> (I, 339)

The more serious of the satiric poems always contain a sense
of moral indignation, sometimes moral outrage. Like other satir-
ists, Cummings sometimes makes use of scatalogy and the so-called
four-letter Anglo-Saxon words to communicate his outrage. Here
the outrage is directed at war, generally; more specifically, though,
it is not war that is such hell, but the people who play at war
games: the officers, products of socalled military schools; the non-
commissioned officers; the enlisted men; and, above all, their com-
mander-in-chief, the President of the United States. Nor is society
spared; it is suggested in the closing lines that Olaf, whose name
tells the reader that he was probably either foreign-born or a first-
generation American, was braver than many citizens doing what
they considered their duty, and blonder (i.e., purer) than other
Americans. The appeal to statistics is somewhat ironic, for Cummings normally had no use for them.

Olaf is an early type of the individual in Cummings' poems.
While "mostpeople" are content to do their duty, even a duty
carried out when the laws and conventions are suspended, individuals perform the most heroic of tasks: they remain themselves.
In two poems written before he had explained the concept "mostpeople," Cummings had developed the notion that negation of the
individual, which often goes hand in hand with prohibition of a
sort, represents death. Its earliest poetic appearance was in terms
of the grammatical category most often dealing with necessity
and prohibition. It concerns little Effie, whose brains are filled

with gingerbread—six crumbs, whose names (they speak in turn, identifying themselves as they do so) are *may, might, should, could, would,* and *must.* The "six subjunctive crumbs" are, then, the modal auxiliaries of English. Dealing with necessity and prohibition as they do, they represent death. The truth about Effie is not that she's dead; she's simply never been alive (I, 117–118).

The second of the poems, No. 29 of *No Thanks,* makes a related assertion:

most(people

simply

can't)
won't(most
parent people mustn't

shouldn't)most daren't

(sortof people well
youknow kindof)
aint

&

even
(not having
most ever lived

people always)don't

die(becoming most
buried unbecomingly
very

by

most)people
(I, 412)

As if in defense of the assertion, the volume also contained several portraits of such unpeople. One is described who "does

not have to feel because he thinks/ (the thoughts of others, be it
understood)" (I, 406). All might be characterized thus:

> worshipping Same
> they squirm and they spawn
> and a world is for them;whose
> death's to be born)
> (I, 439)

Cummings affirms his belief in individuals most strongly in the
poems about love and lovers. These poems are filled with a kind
of joyous affirmation that is achieved partly through an increasingly skillful use of Cummings' specialized conceptual vocabulary
and partly through that "precision of movement" which he always
valued so highly. As has been noted earlier, Cummings never
altered his basic concerns much; he modified his view of the universe and his approach to it, but he continued to exalt love and
the individual. In modifying his metaphysic, he was careful to
define his terms: the genuine human being can be distinguished
from the docile slave of western technology who most resembles
a "transcendentally sterilized lookiesoundiefeelietastiesmellie" (II,
461), i.e., a sort of ultimate consumer whose attention is so
riveted on his standard of living that he has no time to live. This
contrast is poignantly depicted in one of the best known of Cummings' poems. An exquisitely harmonious lyrical celebration of
love, it is one of his finest poems of this type:

> anyone lived in a pretty how town
> (with up so many floating bells down)
> spring summer autumn winter
> he sang his didn't he danced his did.
>
> Women and men(both little and small)
> cared for anyone not at all
> they sowed their isn't they reaped their same
> sun moon stars rain
>
> children guessed(but only a few
> and down they forgot as up they grew
> autumn winter spring summer)
> that noone loved him more by more

when by now and tree by leaf
she laughed his joy she cried his grief
bird by snow and stir by still
anyone's any was all to her

someones married their everyones
laughed their cryings and did their dance
(sleep wake hope and then)they
said their nevers they slept their dream

stars rain sun moon
(and only the snow can begin to explain
how children are apt to forget to remember
with up so floating many bells down)

one day anyone died i guess
(and noone stooped to kiss his face)
busy folk buried them side by side
little by little and was by was

all by all and deep by deep
and more by more they dream their sleep
noone and anyone earth by april
wish by spirit and if my yes.

Women and men(both dong and ding)
summer autumn winter spring
reaped their sowing and went their came
sun moon stars rain
(II, 515)

Here, in what might almost be called a parable, is the narrative
of "anyone" and "noone." The skillful use of shifted grammatical
forms allows Cummings to charge words with great intensity of
meaning. He does so, here and elsewhere, without making use of
what has been the favorite poetic device of the twentieth century
—that is the frequent use of allusion. A performance like Eliot's
in *The Waste Land* is unthinkable in connection with Cummings.
The referents here are universally understood—no reader could
fail to understand the symbolic meanings of the seasons of the
year, the weathers of the seasons, the significance of the names
and identifications in the poem. One's reading of the poem is

enriched, to be sure, if one understands that Cummings occasionally alludes to his own use of some of the words in special ways
in other poems—though even that is kept to a minimum in this
poem. It does not take much special knowledge to understand that
in this poem positive values and actions are being extolled over
negative ones, and that private happiness is better than shared
lack of awareness. The syntax appears distorted, but is really only
slightly re-arranged, mostly in the interests of metrical harmony.
To render line two in normal word order, for instance, requires
only that we revise it to read "with so many bells floating up
down." The revision destroys the meter and fails to clarify the
meaning; in fact, it confuses it. Normal word order in English, the
pattern whereby most clauses are arranged subject-verb-object (or
-modifier or -complement), presupposes certain things about the
relationship of time and space that we know to be false sometimes. One duty of the artist is to wrench from the medium he
works with a more adequate picture of the universe than convention reveals.

Seasonal imagery is always important in Cummings' poetry.
The general nature of its importance was commented on in a letter
by Cummings. In 1959 he explained this as follows:

> seem to remember asserting that all my bookofpoems after the
> original T&C manuscript—published as Tulips & Chimneys, AND,XLI
> Poems—start with autumn(downgoing,despair)& pass through winter
> (mystery, dream)& stop in spring(upcoming,joy). But as I glance
> over the index of Poems '23–'54, find few hints of this progression;
> beyond a tendency to begin dirty(world: sordid,satires)& end clean
> (earth: lyrical,lovepoems). 95 Poems is,of course,an obvious example
> of the seasonal metaphor—1,a falling leaf;41,snow;73,nature(whole-
> ness innocence eachness beauty the transcending of time&space)
> awakened. "Metaphor" of what? Perhaps of whatever one frequently
> meets via my old friend S.FosterDamon's William Blake/His Philoso-
> phy and Symbols;e.g.(p. 225)"They" the angels "descend on the
> material side . . . and ascend on the spiritual;this is . . . a representa-
> tion of the greatest Christian mystery,a statement of the secret
> which every mystic tries to tell" (*Selected Letters*, p. 261)

A similar rhythmical urge is the informing spirit of the title
poem of *1 × 1*, "if everything happens that can't be done." It is
a beautiful celebration of growth and movement, depending

heavily on Cummings' use of his conceptual vocabulary, and it contains the kind of phrasal repetition that was first introduced in *50 Poems*. It explains the title of the volume in which it is found in a way that no single poem has done in any preceding volume:

> if everything happens that can't be done
> (and anything's righter
> than books
> could plan)
> the stupidest teacher will almost guess
> (with a run
> skip
> around we go yes)
> there's nothing as something as one
>
> one hasn't a why or because or although
> (and buds know better
> than books
> don't grow)
> one's anything old being everything new
> (with a what
> which
> around we come who)
> one's everyanything so
>
> so world is a leaf so tree is a bough
> (and birds sing sweeter
> than books
> tell how)
> so here is away and so your is a my
> (with a down
> up
> around again fly)
> forever was never till now
>
> now i love you and you love me
> (and books are shuter
> than books
> can be)
> and deep in the high that does nothing but fall
> (with a shout
> each

90

around we go all)
there's somebody calling who's we

we're anything brighter than even the sun
(we're everything greater
than books
might mean)
we're everyanything than believe
(with a spin
leap
alive we're alive)
we're wonderful one times one
(II, 594)

Interestingly, that particular poem may not remain a nonce form. It has been used by at least one other poet, an amateur who paid tribute to the memory of Cummings in a poem entitled "IF EDWARD ESTLIN'S IN HEAVEN NOW."

Cummings felt very strongly that "noone who hopes to write poetry should attempt what used to be called free verse until he or she has mastered the conventional forms" (*Selected Letters*, p. 234); he himself mastered the traditional forms early, though the only ones he continued to write with any degree of regularity after the *Tulips and Chimneys* manuscript were sonnets, various kinds of satirical poems, and rhymed and metrical quatrains. The sonnets are an extremely important category of Cummings' poems, both because of the number he wrote and because of their quality. Further, they are of interest because they show the extent to which Cummings was able to experiment with and vary a traditional form. His accomplishment in the sonnet ranges from fairly regular and highly metrical Shakesperian sonnets to such typographically eccentric sonnets that they are often identified as irregular free verse poems.

In terms of quantity, the significance of the sonnets does drop after the *Tulips and Chimneys* manuscript—there were 61 sonnets out of 150 poems, a proportion of about forty per cent—but remains significantly high in the succeeding volumes, particularly the very last ones. Out of a total of 584 poems in nine volumes, one hundred and nineteen poems are sonnets. That represents close to one-fifth of Cummings' published poems after *Tulips and Chimneys*.

Since there is so much variety in Cummings' handling of the sonnet form, it might appear advantageous to divide the sonnets into two groups for discussion, those incorporating many non-traditional features—lack of meter, irregular stanza form, unusual spacing, unorthodox rhyme schemes, exaggerated placement of the turn—and those which adhere to a metrical pattern which makes them easily recognizable as sonnets. They are all sonnets, however, and it would be awkward to try to decide just where to draw the line between the two groups, so they will be treated together.

In examining Cummings' sonnets, there is good reason to do so partly in chronological terms, for the early ones are distinguished from the late ones in a number of interesting and significant ways, both in subject matter and form—so much so that form often correlates with subject matter and the one predicts the other. Before looking at the sonnets themselves, it may be well to underscore what has already been said of Cummings' reverence for form by looking at some of his statements regarding the sonnet as a form. His sense of iconoclasm was such that he surely enjoyed the fact that "Cambridge ladies"—and others—sometimes failed to recognize his sonnets for what they were. Nonetheless, his informing idea was fairly standard, as he once made clear in a letter to a correspondent; he thanked him for a recent poem, then added that he would not call it a sonnet, because for him the word "sonnet" implied "a poem of 14 iambic pentameters, none of them unrhymed." (*Selected Letters*, p. 262) Further, he was certainly aware of the fact that a paraphrase can be a useful reading tool. He received many letters from readers asking him to explain poems or parts of poems; frequently, his response was to explain that while he was not a critic, he would suggest a paraphrase. He once, for instance, gave a detailed paraphrase of this sonnet:

> sonnet entitled how to run the world)
>
> A always don't there B being no such thing
> for C can't casts no shadow D drink and
>
> E ear of her voice in whose silence the music of spring
> lives F feel opens but shuts understand
> G gladly forget little having less
>
> with every least each most remembering
> H highest fly only the flag that's furled

(sestet entitled grass is flesh or swim
who can and bathe who must or any dream
means more than sleep as more than know means guess)

I item i immaculately owe
dying one life and will my rest to these

children building this rainman out of snow
(I, 390)

Cummings preceded his paraphrase with the statement that the poem's first line, semi-parenthetically its title, tells one that the subject of the sonnet is "how to run the world." He then explains that a sonnet has two parts, the octave consisting of eight lines, and the sestet consisting of six lines. He then paraphrases the octave, not line by line but section by section, the new sections being announced by the capital letters in alphabetical order, A through H. He suggests the paraphrase is roughly as follows: The way to run the world is always not to try to run it. Since the apparently real world is actually an illusion, that is, something negative or lacking substance, one should, instead of worrying about worldly things, drink and eat of the earth's substance. Above all, one should remember that to feel is an opening experience, while to understand is a shutting experience. Also one should never be guilty of self-pity, but be happy with the moment. Finally, one should treat his highest self as something sacred, never flaunting it in public. The paraphrase of the sestet suggests that lines 9, 10, and 11 say that the subject of the second part of the poem is not that "flesh is grass (i.e., living is dying) as the Bible says, but that dying is living ("grass is flesh"). That notion can also be expressed by saying that what's important is not conforming, but self-expression, or that dreaming matters more than sleeping, and guessing is more important than knowing. The very last part of the poem, says Cummings, can be paraphrased by saying

> I owe death one life,the mortal part of me,& bequeath all the (immortal)rest of myself to these children;whom I see building,out of snow,the figure of a man who'll melt away in the rain(becoming a rainman). (*Selected Letters*, pp. 270–271)

Cummings' comments are revealing. From what he says it appears, first of all, that the capital letters which appear in the poem are strictly visual devices. Second, within the framework of the sonnet form, it is obviously possible to use a conceptual vocabulary together with a very abbreviated syntax in order to achieve an effect almost like that of a typograph. Metrically, this poem is highly irregular; Cummings wrote this poem when he was still experimenting freely with the meter of the sonnet. The sonnet form itself is disarranged, and the rhyme is irregular. However, there is a clear break in the poem at the traditional place, and there is more reason to call it a sonnet than not to. Always, in fact, Cummings' sonnets can be identified as sonnets because they retain a certain number of characteristic features of the form. His irregular sonnets, in other words, are not sonnets because that is what he called them, but because they have the essential shape of the form. The conventional rhyme scheme may go in one, the placement of the turn in another, but always the poem is distinguishable as a sonnet. It is almost as though Cummings' continued experimentation with the form was done with the intention of defining by discovery the quintessential sonnet.

In the following sonnet, for instance, the organization appears to be quite unorthodox. The most important "turn," so far as meaning is concerned, occurs between the thirteenth and fourteenth lines, the first thirteen lines being the text of a speech by a politician making an appeal to the jingoistic proclivities of his audience. Line fourteen then defines the situation: the politician, hot and thirsty, pauses for a drink of water. The poem is composed of what have become meaningless patriotic cliches:

> "next to of course god america i
> love you land of the pilgrim's and so forth oh
> say can you see by the dawn's early my
> country 'tis of centuries come and go
> and are no more what of it we should worry
> in every language even deafanddumb
> thy sons acclaim your glorious name by gorry
> by jingo by gee by gosh by gum
> why talk of beauty what could be more beaut-
> iful than these heroic happy dead
> who rushed like lions to the roaring slaughter
> they did not stop to think they died instead
> then shall the voice of liberty be mute?"

94

> He spoke.   And drank rapidly a glass of water
> (I, 268)

And yet if we examine the rhyme scheme, we find that it divides
the poem into two quatrains, together making an acceptable
octave, and a sestet, rhyming *efgfeg*. And the structural turn does
correspond to a shift in meaning between lines eight and nine, for
line nine begins a rhetorical question which continues through
line thirteen. The central irony of the poem emerges in those
lines: we are hearing neither talk of beauty nor the voice of
liberty. The meter is sometimes irregular, and there is a peculiar
word division at the end of one line, but those irregularities do not
disqualify it as a sonnet.

Thematically, the poem is satire directed at one of Cummings'
favourite targets, politicians. Satire was not to remain the characteristic tone of Cummings' sonnets. The later ones tend to be love
poems of one sort or another, and they increasingly present a
vision of the world in which transcendental values, often expressed
in Cummings' conceptual vocabulary, are seen to be most significant. They are poems in which ideal actions and attitudes are
expressed in terms of positive actions and in which there is also
increased control of both vision and technique. Affirmative action
is sometimes effectively translated into metaphor, as in the one
beginning "here's to opening and upward, to leaf and to sap."
(I, 424)

Love itself is often defined in terms of its functions, as in this
one, which also explains why lovers are the most fortunate of
human beings:

> love's function is to fabricate unknownness
>
> (known being wishless;but love,all of wishing)
> though life's lived wrongsideout,sameness chokes oneness
> truth is confused with fact,fish boast of fishing
>
> and men are caught by worms(love may not care
> if time totters,light droops,all measures bend
> nor marvel if a thought should weigh a star
> —dreads dying least;and less,that death should end)
>
> how lucky lovers are(whose selves abide
> under whatever shall discovered be)

whose ignorant each breathing dares to hide
more than most fabulous wisdom fears to see

(who laugh and cry)who dream,create and kill
while the whole moves;and every part stands still:
(I, 446)

The form here is so unusual as to make this poem initially unrecognizable as a sonnet. Close examination, however, reveals that
the fourteen lines are divided into the familiar three quatrains and
final couplet of a Shakesperian sonnet. The rhyme is absolutely
regular. In two instances, Cummings does substitute a form of half
rhyme or slant rhyme for true rhyme. In the first quatrain, -*known-
ness* rhymes with *oneness*, and in the second quatrain, -*care*
rhymes with *star*. These are both examples of consonance, a form
of rhyme which is not particularly unusual. The meter is fairly
regular.

By contrast, the form of the next sonnet is in some ways even
more unconventional than earlier ones tended to be. For instance,
it makes rather free use of imperfect rhyme. The rhyme scheme
of the first quatrain makes use of consonance in its rhyming of
hearts and *asserts*, with their different stressed vowels, while that
of the second quatrain departs even further from true rhyme by
rhyming *strive* and *love*, *pretend* and *mind*, both more extreme examples of consonance. In the sestet, the rhymed pairs are *now* and
grow, which, strictly speaking, are not rhymes at all; -*where* and
are, another example of consonance; and *was* and *yes*, best thought
of as consonance plus a touch of assonance, since the final conso-
nants differ only in that one is a voiced spirant, *z*, while the other
is its voiceless correspondent, *s*. These departures from true rhyme
so pervade the poem, however, that they must be assumed deliberate. They become, then, an unconventional convention being used
in the sonnet. In other important ways, the sonnet is conventional.
The meter is fairly regular, with only familiar sorts of variation:

> true lovers in each happening of their hearts
> live longer than all which and every who;
> despite what fear denies,what hope asserts,
> what falsest both disprove by proving true
>
> (all doubts,all certainties,as villains strive
> and heroes through the mere mind's poor pretend

96

—grim comics of duration: only love
immortally occurs beyond the mind)

such a forever is love's any now
and her each here is such an everywhere,
even more true would truest lovers grow
if out of midnight dropped more suns than are

(yes;and if time should ask into his was
all shall,their eyes would never miss a yes)
(II, 576)

Of greater interest than the irregularities of form, though, is the picture presented of "lovers" as they are different from "all which" and "very who." There is a clear dichotomy between eternal life —"only love/immortally occurs beyond the mind)"—and the "mere mind's poor pretend." When head and heart are opposed, heart wins.

This romantic distinction between head and heart is one for which Cummings was often unfairly criticized. Certainly, it is true that life seldom offers a clear-cut choice between the two; that, however, is no reason not to have—and give—an opinion about the superiority of one to the other. Those who accuse Cummings of being simplistic in his approach to life are either ignoring poems in which he exhibits great familiarity with the stupidities and excesses of which man is capable or else failing to understand exactly what Cummings meant by his statements. One must know exactly what Cummings meant by "mankind" in order to understand the following poem, which makes a rather strong comment on man's tendency to subvert natural functions:

when serpents bargain for the right to squirm
and the sun strikes to gain a living wage—
when thorns regard their roses with alarm
and rainbows are insured against old age

when every thrush may sing no new moon in
if all screech-owls have not okayed his voice
—and any wave signs on the dotted line
or else an ocean is compelled to close

when the oak begs permission of the birch
to make an acorn—valleys accuse their

mountains of having altitude—and march
denounces april as a saboteur

then we'll believe in that incredible
unanimal mankind(and not until)
(II, 620)

In this poem Cummings is *not* suggesting that serpents have no "right to squirm" or that the sun should not have "a living wage" —or, by extension, that man has no right to certain living conditions. What he *is* suggesting is that man, alone of all the natural phenomena in the world, is capable of so organizing his society that he sometimes has to bargain for the "right to squirm" and has to strike to "gain a living wage." This poem has been subject to some serious and quite unnecessary misunderstanding, most recently by Kenneth R. Attaway, whose *E. E. Cummings' Aloofness: An Underlying Theme in the Poetry* makes the rather extraordinary statement that in the volume from which this poem is taken "Cummings reiterated his refusal to accept mankind on any terms other than his own. 'When serpents bargain for the right to squirm' (*Xaipe*, 1950) makes the statement that the poet will not believe in mankind until nature reverses her laws" (p. 22). It is not human beings that Cummings "refuses to accept"; it is the collective entity "mankind" that he does not "believe" in. The word "believe" also needs comment. Cummings could mean that he doesn't think "mankind" exists. More likely an interpretation, however, is that he does not think that "mankind" has anything to do with human beings. Or, as he said in his "introduction" to *Collected Poems*, "—it's no use trying to pretend that mostpeople and ourselves are alike. Mostpeople have less in common with ourselves than the squarerootofminusone." (II, 461)

Formally, this sonnet exhibits features which have become familiar to the readers of Cummings' sonnets. The three quatrains and final couplet make abundant use of various kinds of half rhyme. The meter is good solid iambic pentameter, with no particularly jarring variations. The rhetorical patterning of the poem, a series of "when" clauses followed by a result clause (here introduced by "then") is one that Cummings used several times in poems. The reader may want to look at another one, "when faces called flowers float out of the ground". (II, 665)

An appropriate last sonnet for examination here is one from the volume published posthumously, *73 Poems*. The transcendental affirmation of the poem combined with the theme of approaching darkness results in a poem of prayer, unusual in Cummings' *oeuvre*. The form of the sonnet is fairly relaxed; the odd arrangement corresponds to that relaxed quality:

> Now i lay(with everywhere around)
> me(the great dim deep sound
> of rain;and of always and of nowhere)and
>
> what a gently welcoming darkestness—
>
> now i lay me down(in a most steep
> more than music)feeling that sunlight is
> (life and day are)only loaned:whereas
> night is given(night and death and the rain
>
> are given;and given is how beautifully snow)
>
> now i lay me down to dream of(nothing
> i or any somebody or you
> can begin to begin to imagine)
>
> something which nobody may keep.
> now i lay me down to dream of Spring
>   (II, 816)

Of the other fixed forms Cummings continued to write, satires and other poems employing rhymed couplets or quatrains are relatively frequent. The subjects of the satires are most often politicians and literary figures. One of the most effective of the latter is one written in honor of Louis Untermeyer, who had once put together an anthology of modern American poetry striking for its omission of William Carlos Williams and Marianne Moore and for its inclusion of Louis Untermeyer:

> mr u will not be missed
> who as an anthologist
> sold the many on the few
> not excluding mr u
>   (II, 551)

99

Cummings' attitude toward politicians, generally, is summed up in this couplet:

> a politician is an arse upon
> which everyone has sat except a man
> (II, 550)

It is strange, at first glance, to see that Cummings objects as seriously to politicians operating in capitalistic societies as he does to those operating in the Communist world. Yet he does. If "kumrads die because they're told)" (I, 413), they are not vastly different from those who live in the "land of the Cluett/ Shirt Boston Garter and Spearmint/ Girl with the Wrigley Eyes" (I, 230); the question is not one of systems, but of attitudes: "A world of made is not a world of born—". (II, 554)

It would be possible to arrange a kind of reverse hierarchy of Cummings' values, on which could be placed, in descending order of size and abstraction, the "gangs, groups, and collectivities" to which Cummings objected. At the top would be "mostpeople." Just below would be, perhaps, two large groups: Westerners, who suffer the "comfortable disease" called "Progress" (II, 554), and Russian Marxists, who live under a system where "moscow pipes good kumrads dance)" (I, 413). Below these two groups would be other, smaller ones. In America, the groups represented would certainly include politicians, salesmen, missionaries, etc., while in Russia one would expect to see represented the "Gay-Pay-Oo" and other official organizations.

Some readers have taken exception to what has seemed—to them, though not to all readers—racism in Cummings' poems. The one below has bothered many readers, particularly because he himself seemed fond of it. He wrote to a correspondent once that he was pleased he had liked this one and another ("a kike is the most dangerous"), because a "friend and critic" had once tried to dissuade him from including them in *Xaipe*, on the ground that the words "nigger" and "kike" would hurt some sensitive readers and prejudice them against the book (*Selected Letters*, p. 210). Here is the first poem:

> one day a nigger
> caught in his hand
> a little star no bigger
> than not to understand

100

"i'll never let you go
until you've made me white"
so she did and now
stars shine at night
(II, 622)

Contemporary readers are quite likely to agree with Cummings'
"friend and critic" that the poem is in questionable taste, to say
the least. The word "nigger" as it is used in this poem is certain
to bring forth the charge "racist!" from many readers. Further,
the poem seems to imply that being white is more desirable than
being black, and that opinion is by no means a universal one.
What seems to be true about this poem, though, is not that it
reveals Cummings to be a racist, but that it shows how faulty his
critical judgment could sometimes be in reference to his own work.
For he has obviously failed to communicate what he was trying to
communicate. His aim in the poem, he once wrote Friedman, was
to expose "do-goodery." Stars once shone in the daytime as well
as at night. A black who resented his blackness complained. A star
attempted to "rescue" the black man from his condition by acquiesc-
ing in his demand and turning him white—i.e., middle-class and
respectable. That action represented a kind of condescension. Now
stars shine only at night. As Friedman has suggested, the tale is
too condensed and cryptic.

The same thing might be said about another poem in the same
volume (*Xaipe*), one which raised quite a furor, because it led to a
charge of anti-Semitism when Cummings was awarded a Fellowship of the Academy of American Poets in 1950. The poem
objected to read as follows:

a kike is the most dangerous
machine as yet invented
by even yankee ingenu
ity(out of a jew a few
dead dollars and some twisted laws)
it comes both prigged and canted
(II, 644)

It is certainly possible, as more than one critic has pointed out in
no uncertain terms, to read this poem as an example of the most
rabid sort of anti-Semitism. The charge made is serious enough,

in fact, that one entire section of the first collection of critical essays about Cummings was devoted exclusively to the question of anti-Semitism in his poetry. The book is S. V. Baum's *EΣTI: eec: E. E. Cummings and the Critics* (1962); seven of its thirty-two essays are found in the section "Anti-Semitism and E. E. Cummings: A Critical Round Robin." The most unsympathetic comments about Cummings are to be found in an essay by Stanton A. Coblentz, "He is a vicious Anti-semite." In it the charge is made that Cummings is socially vicious and that he uses

> the language of racial bias, the same outrageous racial bias as was responsible for the circulation in Europe of the infamous *Protocols of the Elders of Zion*, and that was not only instrumental in precipitating pograms but that was the central factor behind the bloodiest massacre in known history: the Hitlerite slaughter of the defenseless Jews of Europe. (Baum, p. 178)

That is a very serious charge, the more so because Coblentz implies strongly that using the language of racial bias is tantamount to being racially biased. That by no means follows. As Alex Jackinson points out, in "The Question Posed," offending words or lines must be judged on the basis of how they are used in context:

> Cummings, it must always be stressed, makes poetry out of the nomenclature of the street; the gutter, if one wishes. In each of his many books one can find enough slang and colloquialisms to make the squeamish blush. He has poems in the Italian dialect, poems that satirize the English (Lord John Unalive), and others that rip into Finklesteins. To him nothing is sacred. This may still not excuse his poking fun at Jews, but when viewed (as it should be viewed) as a part of Cummings' larger mural of peans and prejudices, it is his collective good taste more than his anti-Semitism which becomes suspect. (Baum, pp. 174–175)

Cummings himself has made a telling comment on the poem. Charles Norman records that it was made in response to a question he posed:

> I asked Cummings: "What is the real meaning of poem 46 in *Xaipe*? Is it reaction to a particular individual?" He replied:
> "I feel that a poem 'means' differently for each individual who

encounters it, but which (if any) of its 'meanings' deserve to be called the 'real' one, I don't know. All I can even try to tell you is what this poem means as far as I'm concerned.

"Whereas in unpopular parlance, 'a kike' equals a jew, for me 'a kike' equals an UNjew. Why? Because for me a jew is a human being;whereas 'a kike' is a machine—the product of that miscalled Americanization; alias standardization(id est dehumanization) which from my viewpoint, makes out&out murder a relatively respectable undertaking." (*E. E. CUMMINGS: The Magic-Maker*, p. 319)

Though no reader is obliged to find in the poem the same "meaning" that Cummings did, he is bound to take into consideration what the author has said and to be aware of the reasons some critics have seen in the poem a similar "meaning." It is possible to see the poem as being not anti-Semitic at all, but pointedly anti-anti-Semitic.

A further serious objection to the poem is that it concludes with a kind of Prufrock-like squeamishness about human sexuality. The squeamishness is greatly multiplied if one knows that the last line originally read "it comes both pricked and cunted." The substitution was made because of a publisher's reluctance to print the original words; interestingly, the linguistic patterning seems to retain the original semantic effect. All in all, the poem has little more to recommend it than the one discussed earlier. Poets do nod.

For all the fuss and fury, there seems little evidence that Cummings was racist or anti-Semitic on principle. There is no reason, certainly, to think that blacks and Jews belong on the reverse hierarchy of Cummings' values. To read that into his poetry is to misunderstand him. Satire was certainly involved in each of the poems discussed above. It was not, however, blacks and Jews who were being satirized. The person being satirized in the first poem is the black who wants to be white; in the second poem, more bitter in its judgment, the person being satirized is the White Anglo-Saxon Protestant who conjures up a bogeyman of whom he must then be afraid. In the situation that inevitably ensues, the Jew certainly suffers. Cummings does not suggest otherwise. The reader who is bothered by Cummings' use of words like "kike" and "nigger"—and, elsewhere, "wop" and "yeggs" and "thirsties"— would do well to remember that avoidance of the language of racial bias has never perceptibly altered the degree of racial bias in the world.

Not all Cummings' experiments with rhymed couplets and quatrains were in the vein of satire. One very late poem—in *95 Poems*—is interesting as an example of the other uses to which Cummings could put his talents in the couplet. It also serves as an example of an exercise in ambiguity not often characteristic of his poems. It demonstrates effectively the way in which the outer self is a clue to the inner self, and it does so with great apparent simplicity of language and surface meaning:

> maggie and milly and molly and may
> went down to the beach(to play one day)
>
> and maggie discovered a shell that sang
> so sweetly she couldn't remember her troubles,and
>
> milly befriended a stranded star
> whose rays five languid fingers were;
>
> and molly was chased by a horrible thing
> which raced sideways while blowing bubbles: and
>
> may came home with a smooth round stone
> as small as a world and as large as alone.
>
> For whatever we lose(like a you or a me)
> it's always ourselves we find in the sea
> (II, 682)

The vocabulary here is deceptively simple; only in the final couplet is there any use of Cummings' conceptual vocabulary. And the form is neither obscure nor puzzling; as a result, the surface level meaning is so obvious that it almost immediately becomes secondary to the structure and imagery, which are much stronger elements in the poem. The poem is also rich in several types of ambiguities. Structure re-enforces meaning at every point. The fourth couplet, for instance, that about molly, is the only one which has neither true rhyme nor imperfect rhyme; it thus emphasizes the disharmony of molly's soul. That lack of humanity is in keeping with the order of presentation of the vowels in the four names, each beginning with the sound *m*; the vowel sounds in the

four names move from front to back till molly's name is mentioned, and then suddenly there is a jump to the far front for the
successful may. The word *chased* is a deliberate pun, hinting at
molly's repressions, which burst out in their "horrible" vision;
"raced" echoes "rays" of the preceding couplet, and "sideways"
rhymes with it, but the dentals add an element of harshness carried through into the final labials. This rhyme and the consonance
of "sang" and "thing," as well as the rough rhythm in these two
lines, suggest a basic parallel between maggie's case and that of
molly—though the former escapes through art. May's experience
is the only one presented in true rhyme; roundness suggests the
self-contained completeness of her experience. It also reminds one
of the Buddhist Wheel of Life—and, in addition, is, of course,
a sexual symbol.

The poem is a deliberate study in awareness; its artistic merit
derives from the subtle complexities of sound and meaning. Each
syllable, each phoneme has a definite part in the unity of the
whole, and the nuances of meaning derive as much from the
functions of rhyme and position as from the emotional and intellectual conceptions embodied in the poem.

Some of Cummings' poems do not fit neatly into any classification scheme. Omitted thus far, for instance, has been any mention of his deliberately anti-romantic poems, in the tradition of
Shakespeare's "My Mistress' eyes are nothing like the sun." One
of the earliest examples is one of the new poems in *&* [*AND*]. The
closing lines, given here, illustrate the kind of thing Cummings did
in those poems:

> your expression
> > my love
> > > when most passionate.,
> > > > my,love
> is thatofa   fly.pre cisel   Yhalf
>
> (squashe)d
>
> > with,its,little,solemn,   entrails
> (I, 94)

✳ The truth is that it is impossible to classify Cummings' poems
on the basis of any single classification scheme. He was a lyric

105

poet whose range was extraordinary. He greatly enlarged the boundaries of the possible where the lyric was concerned. His accomplishments in the lyric ranged from the highly melodic—a number of his poems have been set to music, some of them more than once—to the literally unpronounceable. Many of his individual volumes of poems give, in miniature, a picture of the range of his interests and visions and talents. Frequently, the poems are set within a kind of framework in which the first poem is a typograph of some sort, while the final poem of the volume is a love poem in some traditional form, often a sonnet. Since Cummings was painstaking in his attention to the arrangement of his poems, it is surely noteworthy that this framework is used, and that it is within such a framework that the various poems occur. There is a move from a celebration of the moment, with its accompanying metaphysical implications, to an ordered and orderly picture of the universe. Form implies meaning, and the progression is significant: "love is the whole and more than all" (II, 521).

Readers who have found in Cummings' work an apparent preponderance of romantic love or indignation should remember that the turn of a page may bring with it the reverse of the coin. Great love for individuals often goes hand in hand with a large capacity for moral outrage at their ill-treatment. Cummings was not a man for all seasons, nor are his poems a storehouse of "something for everyone." He was, however, a man who genuinely loved men and the craft of poetry and hated those things which make men less than men and poetry mere words. That is sufficient to recommend him to the ages.

4

The Prose

E. E. Cummings' prose works are as original and as exciting as the best of his poems. In fact, Cummings felt that his identity as a writer lay in prose as much as in poetry. He said in "nonlecture one" that he found his stance as a writer most clearly expressed in "the later miscalled novel, the two plays, perhaps twenty poems, and half a dozen of the essays" (p. 4). One of the two plays is a prose work—clearly, his prose writings were very important to him. By "the later miscalled novel," he meant *Eimi*; the first one was *The Enormous Room*. To that list might now be added the work from which the above quotation was taken, *i:six non-lectures* (1953).

The prose juvenalia, which occupy much less of the preserved manuscript material than the early poetry, is of interest for what it reveals about Cummings' early interests in character and dialogue. One early story, written when Cummings was fourteen years old, is noteworthy because it is one of the earliest extant manuscripts which demonstrates Cummings' attempts to portray the dialect patterns of rural New England speech. He must have encountered the dialect of uneducated natives of New Hampshire very early, for his parents had purchased the Joy Farm at Silver Lake before Cummings' younger sister was born, and the family apparently spent a part of each summer there. Elizabeth was only a few years younger than Cummings, so he must have been quite young the first time he heard the New Hampshire dialect that was so different from that of his native Cambridge. The epistolary style of Sam Ward, the caretaker at Joy Farm, influenced Cummings' poetic style; the tribute the poet has paid to that influence is substantiated by letters from Ward to members of the

Cummings family. At any rate, the strange dialect seems to have made quite an impression on the young Cummings. The story of "Elizabeth Eliza" is noteworthy for its character differentiation, and that differentiation is achieved primarily by means of dialect.

The main characters in the tale are Elizabeth Eliza and her young brother Johnny, and their adoptive parents, Ma-Jane and Dad-John. Minor characters of importance are an elderly gentleman whom Eliza meets on the street one day and Billy Barton, a neighborhood boy who is Elizabeth's age. Elizabeth herself is an extraordinary figure, a sort of female Horatio Alger who hasn't yet made good. She and Johnny, orphaned early in life, have grown up in a Home. She has never been to school, and she goes to church for the first time in Chapter Three of this work. The story is unfinished; however, there are included in the manuscript two different chapter outlines for the entire book. Completed, it would have been a reasonably well-written juvenile novel. As it stands, it is, among other things, a testament to the thoroughness with which the young writer planned the work.

It is Elizabeth's dialogue that is of greatest interest, partly because there is so much of it. Below are given some of the speeches in which she is clearly (if sometimes crudely and occasionally even wrongly) made to copy the speech of uneducated natives of New Hampshire, as a young boy from Cambridge might have heard it:

> I guess it must o' been God , . . .
> I guess 'o , . . . 'cause I never heard of
> 'is having any other.
> They must be very 'appy.
> I kinder wish. . . .
> I'm sorry I fighted Billy.

Some of this was probably meant to be baby talk, but much of it seems to be meant to represent the rural speech patterns of the characters being portrayed. These examples are backed up by examples of indirect discourse in which the young author has Elizabeth Eliza offer her opinion that "she was five and a twarter, an' John, he was two and a half in Jan'rary and that 'dat made the diffe'nce."

Ma-Jane and Dad-John have few lines of dialogue. Their laconic nature serves to characterize them as New Englanders. The author does work in an occasional "Thar! . . . Thar!" for Ma-Jane, though.

Billly Barton displays dialect characteristics also. His few lines are primarily devoted to an unhappy apology for fighting with Elizabeth. Typical is the line "I'se 'orry I—fighted, . . ."

The use of dialect in the story contrasts sharply with the narrative style of the author, who begins his work with words reminiscent of the "Gentle Reader" school of fiction:

> I am starting in to tell you about Elizabeth Eliza, not her brother Johnny, but as the former was invariably accompanied by the later [sic], my tale may drift, at times, from its subject, and I beg the reader to make suitable allowances for such a mistake on my part.

Immature as the work is, its existence is further evidence of the seriousness with which Cummings early took the craft of writing. Presumably he tried various forms of literature before he later became "irrevocably a poet." The second story, an undated, untitled manuscript, begins "Under the New Hampshire moon the loons' wild laughter. . . ." The story itself is of no great interest; while capably written, it depends too heavily on a contrived reversal of expectation in the plot-line for it to be successful. It does show, though, that the young Cummings was capable of plotting a full-length story and developing his characters in a meaningful way. In the characterization there are touches of caricature that characterize many of the poetic portraits. There is, for instance, a young journalist who is described as being "a lover of the Indian school of romance: to him all women were as scalps."

These are the only existing prose works of any length which predate Cummings' university work. There, the first significant piece of his prose to be published was the text of his Commencement Address on "The New Art," which originally appeared in *The Harvard Advocate* for June, 1915. It can be found in the recent collection, *E. E. Cummings: A Miscellany Revised*, a corrected version of the earlier *Miscellany*, published by Argophile Press in 1958. Both collections were edited by George J. Firmage, the poet's bibliographer. The earlier version was published only in an edition limited to seventy-five signed and less than a thousand unsigned copies, so it is fortunate that the book has been given a second life. It is a collection of shorter pieces by Cummings that had not previously been published in book form by the author. It contains, in fact, all but three known appearances; three stories were omitted at the request of Cummings, who did not consider them successful. Two other items in the collection are early published prose works; one is a loving appreciation of the sculptor Gaston Lachaise, for whose work Cummings had very high regard; the other is a review of *Poems* (1919) by T. S. Eliot. "Gaston Lachaise" marked Cummings' debut as an art critic for *The Dial*, in which periodical "T. S. Eliot" also appeared. In both, he demonstrated continued interest in what he had earlier called the "many branches" of the New Art. Of particular interest in the latter essay are the three reasons for which Eliot's poems are praised: for Eliot's success in remaining outside the Vorticist movement, for the fact that every page impressed Cummings with an "overwhelming sense of technique," and because the sensitivity which results in Eliot's poems is such that dissection is unnecessary. Cummings defined technique at length, first stating what he did *not* mean by it—"a great many things, including: anything static, a school, a slogan, a formula"—and then stating what he *did* mean by it: "the alert hatred of normality which, through the lips of a tactile and cohesive adventure, asserts that nobody in general and some one in particular is incorrigibly and actually alive" (*A Miscellany Revised*, p. 27).

Cummings' work for *The Dial* was interrupted by his unfortunate experiences in France during the war. The events surrounding his arrest and subsequent incarceration are, of course, recorded in his first full-length prose work, *The Enormous Room* (1922). It was Cummings' first book, and it was an incredible *tour de force* that has since taken its place in the view of many readers as one of the most important and most original books to come out of a war experience. Though often referred to as a novel, it is rather a prose rendering, in chronological sequence for the most part, of a journal or notebook which Cummings kept as the events of the book occurred.

Since books never make their appearance in a vacuum, but appear on a particular scene, it will be well to examine the context in which Cummings' first book made its initial appearance. The importance of the year 1922 for literature in the English-speaking world has recently been stressed by an exhibition at the

New York Public Library; entitled "1922: A Vintage Year," it contained collections of manuscripts, letters, drawings, photographs, and first editions from the library's Albert A. and Henry W. Berg collection of English and American literature. The following works of "outstanding quality" appeared in 1922: Joyce's *Ulysses*, T. S. Eliot's *The Waste Land*, the first edition of John Galsworthy's *The Forsyte Saga*, F. Scott Fitzgerald's *The Beautiful and Damned*, Virginia Woolf's *Jacob's Room*, Sinclair Lewis's *Babbitt*, E. M. Forster's *Alexandria: A History and a Guide*, five books of poetry and plays by W. B. Yeats—and *The Enormous Room*. Other, sometimes more popular, works—which appeared that year were Katherine Mansfield's *The Garden Party and Other Stories*, Hilaire Belloc's *The Jews*, James Weldon Johnson's *The Book of American Negro Poetry*, Booth Tarkington's *Gentle Julia*, Carl Van Vechten's *Peter Whiffle*, Arnold Bennett's *Mrs. Prohack*, G. K. Chesterton's *What I Saw in America*, Eugene O'Neill's *The Hairy Ape*, and John Hall Wheelock's *The Black Panther*. It can easily be argued that Cummings' first book gains little from being tossed in with some of the others on the list. The point is that it *was* tossed in with others on the list. For that reason, it is easy to see why *The Enormous Room* suffered relative obscurity for a time. It appeared when a much heavier-handed kind of social comment was expected in America, and of course it was not immediately known in England. And it was occasionally objected to on the grounds that it was not "patriotic." Many reviews were receptive to the insights of the book, however, and its ultimate acceptance as a Modern Library classic (1934) is probably partly a result of that early favourable reception. The book has needed periodic rescuing from neglect, however, and the reasons for that are not completely clear. Some readers may be put off by Cummings' general reputation for being "difficult." The prose of *The Enormous Room* is not difficult, however; certainly that of a poet, it is nonetheless fairly simple and straight-forward, both in form and substance.

The events of the book occurred between August, 1917, and January, 1918. They are narrated in a form that suggests a loose parallel between Cummings' experiences and those related in John Bunyan's *Pilgrim's Progress*. Pilgrim's "progress" was a Christian one; Cummings' is transcendent, if not specifically Christian. His journey begins when he and his friend Slater Brown are arrested and taken to Noyon for questioning. The adventure becomes serious when it quickly becomes evident that Brown is on his way to prison, regardless of anything he says or does. Cummings' implication, initially the result of his association with Brown, grows after his initial interrogation, and he shortly finds himself beginning the pilgrimage which was to result in his spending almost three months in *La Ferté Macé*, the journey to which occupies the first four of the thirteen chapters of the book. The first chapter ends with Cummings being locked into a cell for the first time.

The crash of the cell doors behind him produces an "uncontrollable joy" on Cummings' part; he records that he felt free for the first time in three months. The joy is not dissipated by his immediate discovery that he shares the cell with a mouse and a seldom-emptied rude equivalent of a chamber pot. After two nights there, he is taken out and begins the journey proper, starting with a brisk walk to a train station, then a short journey which ends in yet another night in a small cell. Early morning brings another walk and another train journey, this time through Paris. Cummings asks about his destination and is told "Mah-say," which he mistakenly assumes to be Marseilles. It is not until he reaches the very end of his journey and is deposited in "an extremely small and rather disagreeable town" that he realizes his mistake. He is conducted to what he first takes to be the town *gendarmerie* and goes to sleep, unaware that he has arrived at his destination. His first impression of the enormous room, the eighty by forty oblong shape in which sixty men lived under the most primitive conditions, is recorded at the end of the third chapter. In the final paragraphs he records going to sleep in "a sea of most extraordinary sound," a room in which at least thirty voices, in eleven languages—he says he counted Dutch, Belgian, Spanish, Turkish, Arabian, Polish, Russian, Swedish, German, French, and English—ferociously bombarded him. The final sentences of the chapter set the tone for what is to follow:

> Nor was my perplexity purely aural. About five minutes after lying down I saw (by a hitherto unnoticed speck of light which burned near the doors which I had entered) two extraordinary looking figures—one a well-set man with a big, black beard, the other a consumptive with a bald head and sickly moustache, both clad only in their knee-length chemises, hairy legs naked, feet bare—wander

down the room and urinate profusely in the corner nearest me. This act accomplished, the figures wandered back, greeted with a volley of ejaculatory abuse from the invisible co-occupants of my new sleeping-apartment; and disappeared in darkness.

I remarked to myself that the gendarmes of this gendarmerie were peculiarly up in languages and fell asleep. (*The Enormous Room*, p. 60)

Morning brings the light, a cup of vile coffee, and the news that "Your friend is here." Cummings locates B., as he calls his friend, and begins to sort out the inhabitants of the *Camp de Triage de la Ferté Macé*. The prisoners, arrayed collectively against *Monsieur le Directeur* and his instruments of power, chiefly fear, consisted of two large groups, officially males suspected of espionage and "females of a well-known type *qui se trouvaient dans la zone des armées*." Few prisoners were guilty of any real crime; most of the men in the prison were foreigners, and many of the women were either victims of geography—"inasmuch as the armies of the Allies were continually retreating, the *zone des armées* (particularly in the case of Belgium) was always including new cities, whose *petites femmes* became automatically subject to arrest" (pp. 82–83)—or were perfectly respectable wives of prisoners who preferred living in proximity to their husbands to the questionable freedom of living alone. The quality of life among both groups was necessarily quite sordid; the constant necessity of fighting for survival had a very demoralizing effect on the men and rendered many of them absolutely bestial, particularly at meal-time. The food was predictably bad; Cummings describes his first canteen meal as consisting of "a faintly-smoking urine-colored circular broth in which soggily hung half-suspended slabs of raw potato" and a hunk of bread "almost bluish in color; in taste mouldy, slightly sour" (p. 94). However, there was never enough to satisfy the appetites of the perpetually hungry prisoners. The cry for the noon meal results in an instantaneous transformation before which Cummings stands amazed:

These eyes bubbling with lust, obscene grins, sprouting from contorted lips, bodies unclenching and clenching in unctuous gestures of complete savagery, convinced me by a certain insane beauty. Before the arbiter of their destinies some thirty creatures, hideous and authentic, poised, cohering in a sole chaos of desire; a fluent

113

and numerous cluster of vital inhumanity. As I contemplated this ferocious and uncouth miracle, this beautiful manifestation of the sinister alchemy of hunger, I felt that the last vestige of individualism was about utterly to disappear, wholly abolished in a gambolling and wallowing throb. (p. 91)

Yet individuals survived, almost incredibly, since survival meant not only successfully thwarting the aims of *le Directeur*, but also surviving the unpleasant tactics of an inevitable Judas and his compatriots, willing accomplices of *le Directeur*. By the end of their first day together in the enormous room, Cummings and B. agree that it is "the finest place in the world" (p. 111).

That conviction is re-enforced by Cummings' growing awareness of the special attributes of those individuals who survive, the Delectable Mountains. These are not just survivors; they are individuals who survive and who also maintain a sense of integrity. Cummings is initially attracted to each of them because of values they hold or exemplify which are important to him. The special nature of their survival is first introduced in Chapter Five, which begins with a brief review of the preceding events; this chapter is stylistically interesting because its opening sentence reveals that for all his "experimentation" Cummings has not yet grown out of the "Gentle Reader" school of fiction. In that opening sentence Cummings makes it clear that he regards his second day at *La Ferté Macé* as the beginning of a new period in his progress; a period, he says, which "extends to the moment of my departure and includes the discovery of the Delectable Mountains" (p. 113). Thus Chapters Five through part of Thirteen form the second part of his pilgrimage, during the recalling of which the author demonstrates to his "own satisfaction (if not to anyone else's)" that he was happier in *La Ferté Macé*, with the Delectable Mountains about him, "than the very keenest words can pretend to express" (p. 313).

Four in number, the Delectable Mountains (the name comes from Bunyan's work, of course) occupy one chapter each. They are not, however, the *only* inhabitants honored by a singling-out. Brief portraits of a number of the prisoners are given in Chapter Five, and almost the whole of Chapter Six is devoted to a description of *le Directeur*, known henceforth as Apollyon, and his instruments of power—Fear, Women, and Sunday. Apollyon was the compleat bureaucrat, and he was served by a host of subordinates

114

whose characters ranged from the somewhat lenient to the next to the lowest species of human organism (the lowest, in Cummings' eyes, was the gendarme proper). They were the ones who wielded the weapon Fear.

The women prisoners, who often suffered far greater deprivation and real torture than the men, were used as weapons in this way: the men were forbidden to speak to the women, or even to look at them. But of course it was very easy for the guards to provoke the men into such communication, after which the offender could then be punished.

Sunday was a weapon in and of itself; regular duties were suspended, and the men had more leisure in which to be provoked into committing punishable offenses. Additionally, the day was used to increase the effectiveness of woman as a weapon. In Cummings' words, the day was used by Apollyon thus:

> lest the orinarily tantalizing proximity of *les femmes* should not inspire *les hommes* to deeds which placed the doers automatically in the clutches of himself, his subordinates, and *la punition*, it was arranged that once a week the tantalizing proximity aforesaid should be supplanted by a positively maddening approach to coincidence. Or in other words, *les hommes* and *les femmes* might for an hour or less enjoy the same exceedingly small room, for purposes of course of devotion—it being obvious to Monsieur le Directeur that the representatives of both sexes at La Ferté Macé were inherently of a strongly devotional nature. And lest the temptation to err in such moments be deprived, through a certain aspect of compulsion, of its complete force, the attendance of such strictly devotional services was made optional. (p. 173)

Mercifully, the Sunday aspect of *La Ferté Macé* was always followed by its more pleasant Monday aspect, its everyday routine, the chief attraction of which was the certainty of new arrivals. Whether attractive or disagreeable, they were a novelty, and they sometimes brought in news of the outside world and perhaps even food or cigarettes. But best of all, one of the new ones might turn out to be a Delectable Mountain. The first one encountered by Cummings was a new arrival, a Gypsy known as The Wanderer, whose first action upon reaching the enormous room was to lie upon his *paillasse* and cry bitterly because he had had to sell his favorite horse. He had a family in the women's quarters and a young son with him in the men's quarters. He settled into the pattern of life of the enormous room and was reasonably happy—married prisoners were allowed to spend a part of each day with their wives or families, if they were present—until the French government learned that he was not legally married to the woman he claimed as his wife. Said government then "in its infinite but unskilful wisdom" decided that since the Wanderer were guilty—"of who knows what gentleness, strength, and beauty"—he should suffer as much as possible. Accordingly, he was packed up and sent elsewhere; his family, of course, had to remain behind. "With him disappeared unspeakable sunlight, and the dark, keen, bright strength of the earth" (p. 230).

The second Delectable Mountain was Zulu, an IS whose attributes are described by Cummings as

> limbs' tin grace, wooden wink, shoulderless unhurried body, velocity of a grasshopper, soul up under his arm-pits, mysteriously falling over the ownness of two feet, floating fish of his slimness half a bird. . . . (p. 253).

Next comes Surplice, probably Polish, utterly courageous, utterly religious, utterly ignorant, utterly filthy, utterly curious, and always utterly hungry. He was, of course, the butt of everyone's ridicule. Cast as the heavy, called by such names as "Syph'lis" and "*Chaude-Pisse*, the Pole," he played the part of the fool to perfection. The implications of his being singled out for bullying were not lost on Cummings, who observed that one of the most terrifying aspects of prison life—perhaps institutional life, generally—was the speed and accuracy with which certain basic fundamental psychological laws are put into practice:

> The case of Surplice is a very exquisite example: everyone, of course, is afraid of *les maladies vénériennes*—accordingly, all pick an individual (of whose inner life they know and desire to know nothing, whose external appearance satisfies the requirements of the mind à propos what is foul and disgusting) and, having tacitly agreed upon this individual as a Symbol of all that is Evil, proceed to heap insults upon him and enjoy his very natural discomfiture. . . . (pp. 264–265)

Surplice and The Wanderer are both eventually sent to Précigné, location of the prison for those who are found guilty while at *La Ferté Macé*.

116

The last and in many ways the most formidable of the Delectable Mountains is Jean le Nègre. The only black prisoner to come to the enormous room, he was, of course, of great interest to all the inhabitants. He was very tall and very handsome, also very vain; his trip to prison was occasioned by his having decided one fine day in Paris that he would be even more handsome, and therefore more appealing to women, if he appeared in uniform. Accordingly, he had purchased the necessary attire for appearing decked out as an English captain.

The significance of the Delectable Mountains deserves some comment. The careful reader will quickly become aware that where they are concerned it is clear that Cummings does not believe that cleanliness is next to godliness; indeed, in this book, uncleanliness becomes the virtuous condition. The only physically clean people in it are Apollyon and his cohorts. The prisoners for whom Cummings felt greatest sympathy are physically dirty. Furthermore, they are often unskilled at communicating verbally. No one is quite sure what language Surplice is endeavouring to speak most of the time, and Zulu communicates in no recognizable language. It is with Zulu, however, that Cummings says he experiences perfect communication; he comments thus:

> I have never in my life so perfectly understood (even to the most exquisite nuances) whatever idea another human being desired at any moment to communicate to me, as I have in the case of The Zulu. And if I had one-third the command over the written word that he had over the unwritten and the unspoken—not merely that; over the unspeakable and the unwritable—God knows this history would rank with the deep art of all time. (pp. 238–239)

Clearly there is some inversion of values at play. Neither cleanliness nor perfect articulation are virtues here; interestingly, perfect command of language is associated with the muddle of bureaucracy responsible for Cummings' presence in the enormous room in the first place.

This inversion of values, with its accompanying emphasis on scatology and filth, was probably responsible for the negative response of the book's earliest readers. Even reviewers who praised its first appearance did so "in spite of" what was often called gratuitous filth. It has more recently been recognized that the scatology and the four-letter words play a vital symbolic role in the book; a glance at *Pilgrim's Progress* will serve as a reminder that Pilgrim himself had to endure the Slough of Despond, itself not a very pleasant place. What has not been generally recognized is the more literal role of the scatology and the four-letter words. The prison *was* a very filthy place; after being there a short time Cummings felt—as Henry David Thoreau had once felt—that if the universe were so constructed that his fellow-prisoners should be in prison, then that was where he also belonged. If Cummings had disguised the facts, he would have been guilty of presenting a less than true picture of his experiences at *La Ferté Macé*. The filth is not gratuitous; it is an honest depiction of one inevitable condition of man in a bureaucratic state.

The inevitable descent from the Delectable Mountains leads to the advent of Three Wise Men, members of the commission which came periodically to *La Ferté Macé* to decide on the guilt or innocence of those incarcerated there. It is through their offices that B. and Cummings are eventually released.

What emerges most strongly from the book is Cummings' strong conviction that if one has to go to prison in order to meet Delectable Mountains, then something is very wrong in the world. It is, as we noted above, not a new idea; the fact that its most eloquent expression in earlier American literature was in the writings of Henry David Thoreau reminds one that Cummings was in the line of transcendentalists who have been among America's most important writers. A second idea of great importance is Cummings' expressed awareness that even the most ignorant of the prisoners had virtues which "mostpeople" do not have. Some of these virtues were displayed when, during their last weeks in the enormous room, Cummings and B. spent most of their free time collecting leaves of various colors. These leaves they put into a notebook, along with all the colors they could find on wrappers, labels, and postage-stamps. Although everyone was puzzled by this activity—naturally enough, Cummings says, since not everyone knew that he and B. were simply effecting a study of color itself—all brought additions to the collection. Looking back to that experience, Cummings said later that he wished he had the complete confidence of one-twentieth as many human beings in the city of New York; if he did, he said, then he would not

118

be so inclined to consider The Great American Public as the most aesthetically incapable organization ever created for the purpose of perpetuating defunct ideals and ideas. But of course The Great American Public has a handicap which my friends at La Ferté did not as a rule have—education. Let no one sound his indignant yawp at this. I refer to the fact that, for an educated gent or lady, to create is first of all to destroy—that there is and can be no such thing as authentic art until the *bons trucs* (whereby we are taught to see and to imitate on canvas and in stone and by words this so-called world) are entirely and thoroughly and perfectly annihilated by that vast and painful process of Unthinking which may result in a minute bit of purely personal Feeling. Which minute bit is Art. (p. 307)

The style of *The Enormous Room* is on the whole fairly conventional; as Friedman has pointed out, it is a great deal more conventional than one realizes until it is compared with later prose works, notably *Eimi*. There do occur here and there in the book bits and pieces of prose which more nearly resemble poems than ordinary prose. They are characterized by a wrenching of syntax that renders them in effect asyntactical. The wrenching is deliberate; Cummings was striving to develop not only the notion that conventional use of language is a habit that has to be broken if one is to deal honestly with experience, but also a style—or set of styles—by which that notion could be demonstrated. He does not develop that style—or set of styles—in this book, but he begins the development. Take, for example, the concluding paragraph, the one which puts Cummings back into Manhattan:

The tall, impossibly tall, incomparably tall, city shoulderingly upward into hard sunlight leaned a little through the octaves of its parallel edges, leaningly strode upward into firm, hard, snowy sunlight; the noises of America nearingly throbbed with smokes and hurrying dots which are new and curious and hard and strange and vibrant and immense, lifting with a great ondulous stride firmly into immortal sunlight. . . . (pp. 331–332)

In the decade between the publication of *The Enormous Room* and *Eimi* (1933), Cummings' ability to bend language to his will increased enormously, and to go from the earlier book to the later one is to see at a glance a record of that development. To trace it in greater detail, one should return to the collection of short pieces in *A Miscellany Revised*. Herein are contained the essays he wrote for *The Dial, Vanity Fair*, and a handful of other periodicals during the twenties and early thirties. The short pieces are different from and less successful individually than either *The Enormous Room* or *Eimi*. The difference is that between journalism and art. Each of the full-length books is as much the result of Cummings' total reaction to a series of events as any one of his poems is the result of his total reaction to something. The essays are often journalism—interesting journalism, sometimes, but not art. The difference can be described in many ways. Among other things, it is fair to say that the journalistic essays could be improved in a number of ways. It is easy to imagine that most would have been the better for a period of being put aside, a revision. It is difficult, however, to conceive either *The Enormous Room* or *Eimi* being different from what it is; neither would have been the better for a period of waiting.

The essays are important, though; many are informative and entertaining, and all help to show Cummings' growth as a writer. The main defect of the less interesting ones is a cuteness that quickly wears thin, particularly if it falls at all short of the mark. It is an infrequent indulgence, however; the real wonder of these pieces is not that there is an occasional note of cuteness, but that they do on the whole remain so readable. In addition to the three earlier pieces, there are the following: poems (one in translation), six selections from plays, one "cluster of epigrams" (Cummings' description), the text of one entire book ([*No Title*], 1930), and fifty essays, three in dialogue form. The book thus constitutes a one-volume collection of Cummings' minor prose works. To the material it contains should be added the stories in the 1965 edition of *Fairy Tales*.

Many of the essays purport to be criticism, but they are criticism of a very special type, and they frequently say more about E. E. Cummings than his ostensible subject matter. The essays may be divided on the basis of subject matter into a limited number of groupings. There are fifteen essays on the arts, seven of them having to do specifically with Cummings' art or his view of the role of the artist. Six essays have to do with the circus, burlesque, Coney Island, and the zoo; one long essay is a loving explication of the appeal of the comic series "Krazy Kat"; one group of five essays examines the peculiarities of the French and Italian national temperaments as opposed to that of the United States. The remainder of the essays are satires, the largest number, sixteen, being devoted to social satire; two essays are political satire, and eight are satires on criticism.

The most successful of the essays are those in which there is a perfect blending of style and subject matter. Cummings was not really a critic; in fact, he had little respect for the function of the critic. But he was superb at appreciation and wrote lovingly of subjects that his blood approved. "A Foreword to Krazy," written for a collection of George Harriman's comic strips, is a good example of Cummings' appreciation at its best. He had long been an admirer of the series; in his senior year at Harvard, he had adorned his walls with "Krazy Kat" strips, and he had several times arranged to have them mailed to him in Europe. He saw the situation in "Krazy Kat" as a "meteoric burlesk melodrama" in which love always finds a way. It involves a

> struggle between society (Offissa Pupp) and the individual (Ignatz Mouse) over an ideal (our heroine)—a struggle from which, again and again and again, emerges one stupendous fact; namely, that the ideal of democracy fulfills herself only if, and whenever, society fails to suppress the individual. (*A Miscellany Revised*, p. 327)

The satires are the single most interesting group of essays. Each one explores in brief an aspect of life in the western world. The essays on France and Italy are of particular interest, not only because they introduce a theme which culminates in "Why I Like America," but also because they illuminate the body of social and political satire on life in America which formed such an important part of all Cummings' writings. It is quite clear from these brief essays that what sometimes appears to be criticism of the United States exclusively is in actuality criticism of the western world. That world is extended to include Russia in *Eimi*; one suspects that had Cummings lived longer and traveled wider, it would have included other continents as fast as they were becoming "Americanized." One of the essays, "Conflicting Aspects of Paris," contains social satire as well; in it, Cummings suggests that Paris is the site of a Holy War between the Worshippers of Life and the Worshippers of Bathtubs. Beneath "Gay Paree," the city inhabited by the latter, there continues "Paname," with "a heart that throbs

121

always, a spirit which cannot die" (p. 158). It is Puritans who suffer most in this essay; one is reminded also of the inverted values of the enormous room. As Cummings puts it here:

> Cleanliness is indeed next to godliness! Formerly a vein, *Boulevard Montparnasse* has become an artery through which pulses most of the none-too-red blood which comes straight from the none-too-sound heart of Greenwich Village, U.S.A. God's in His Heaven, prices soar, National Cash Registers adorn all the progressive cafés, Wrigley advertises where it will do most good, the franc touches 22.... (p. 157)

The franc was, of course, much in the news when Cummings was writing these essays. In another one he examines its fall; he concludes, apparently seriously, that

> a certain group of French profiteers, having succeeded in not fighting the war and having partially succeeded in debasing the franc for their own benefit, are now trying to "cover up"—by making, of the erstwhile dearly beloved United States of America, one vast substantial goat. (p. 183)

Notice that it is "French profiteers," not "the French" who come off poorly here. "How I Do Not Love Italy" is identified as being "An extremely unorthodox view of a widely celebrated section of Europe"; it is preceded by a putative "Editor's Note" which is typical of a kind of game-playing which characterized some items in *Vanity Fair* where these essays originally appeared:

> The receipt of this article in the office of Vanity Fair caused a high degree of perturbation and anguish. Why? Because the Editors were nurtured on Italian culture, achievements and ideals. Our first thought, therefore, was that the author of the essay should be reprimanded, not to say chastised. Then there came to us this thought. What if Italy *should* become efficient? What if automats and five-and-ten-cent-stores and slot machines and Ford factories and quick lunch counters should definitely succeed the sonnets of Petrarch, the paintings of Mantegna, the learning of Giovanni Bologna and the large, easy-going, colourful grandeur of the Medicis? Merciful heavens, what weighty pain in that thought! With that direful prospect in mind we saw the need of publishing Mr. Cummings' article forthwith, *in toto*, with the idea of saving Italy from imminent disaster, from modernity, and from (what is most terrifying of all)—American efficiency. (p. 164)

In the essay itself Cummings tells of a series of trips—one by
bicycle from Paris to Naples, one to Rome, a third including
Venice and Florence—which led him from mere disillusionment
at the physical appearance of Italy, to aesthetic shock at the liberties taken with her art—a postcard depicting Mussolini in the role
of Christ, raising *Italia*, in the role of Lazarus, from the dead—to
sleepless enlightenment concerning the Americanization of Italy:

> Assuming the continuation of Italia's present *régime*, America will
> find herself playing second fiddle to *Italia* in more unlovely ways
> than either Napoleon or Caesar could shake a stick at. Already
> *Italia* is up to America's tricks of "progress" and "morality." If you
> doubt this, get in touch with the fascist representative in your home
> town and find out for himself. Already the *Piazza Venezia* is dark
> and dreary. Already you cannot buy a glass of *cognac* on Sunday.
> Later, or sooner, everybody in the "land of beauty, of sunlight and
> song" will be minding everybody else's business as thoroughly as
> everybody else does in the dear old U.S.A.—at least, so your corres-
> pondent decided one night, when (being unable to sleep on account
> of a deafening racket) he lifted up his weary eyes and beheld,
> emblazoned on the door of his microscopic room at the *Albergo*
> Somethingorother, the following moonlit sentiment: *In the generally
> interests, the Visitors are requested to observe the extremely quiet.*
> (p. 168)

The essay "Why I Like America" is identified as being "By an
American who, most unfashionably, prefers his native land to
France"; that identification reveals that one purpose of the essay
is to satirize the current fashion among American intellectuals of
preferring all things French to all things American. Another purpose, though, is to explore positive aspects of America, one of
which is her very size. Without suggesting that America has not
made "prodigious mistakes," has not got "colossal faults," Cummings points out that size may be a virtue, may even be a form of
intensity, a quality almost universally admired. In any contest between size and intensity, the latter always ends. Certainly, as Cummings point out, no one regards a certain painting by Cézanne
as inferior to a certain painting by Sargent just because Sargent's
canvas is larger, anymore than anyone would maintain that the
Brooklyn Bridge is a thousand times more beautiful than the *Pont
Neuf* just because it is a thousand times larger. America might be

many times as large as she is and still be inferior to France. Size and intensity are not always in opposition, however, and as Cummings goes on to say, intensity may be of various kinds. Size may be one kind of intensity, as in the case of skyscrapers, who owe their intensity primarily and fundamentally to their size. Thus this *caveat*:

> Your fashionable brained American, . . . is very fond of twisting the fact that America's bigness has encouraged a lot of drivel into the falsehood that America is drivelling because she is big. One might as well assume that the magnificent ceiling of the Sistine Chapel is a mass of balderdash because the authors of guidebooks use it as an excuse to slop all over themselves. Indeed, like the bigness of the Sistine ceiling, the bigness of America is intrinsic; or, to put the matter a little differently, America is essentially not an enlargement of something else. Her very size is an essential part of her life in the same way that France's culture is an essential part of her life. And this brings the unfashionably brained writer to a full-fledged conviction: he thoroughly believes that America is more alive than France. (p. 195)

To extoll the virtues of size is one thing; to use it to make such a comparison is another. It is impossible to read that last sentence without feeling that Cummings' experiences in France during the first World War lie back of it. And certainly Cummings did not extoll size when he explored in *Eimi* his responses to his trip to Russia.

That book, his second full-length work of prose, bears similarities to *The Enormous Room*; both are records of personal experience, recorded in more-or-less chronological order; both result from a strong conviction, based on personal experience, that there are things desperately wrong in the world; and both are modelled loosely on other literary works, this time *The Divine Comedy*. They are, however, rather different sorts of books. Cummings valued the later book more; his stated conviction that *Eimi* helped explain his stance as a writer is re-enforced by the fact that he devoted a significant part of his sixth lecture at Harvard to comments about and a reading from the book. It is, as he says, "written in a style of its own," and it is admittedly difficult reading.

The very title of the book (Greek for "I am") makes it sound more typically Cummings; increasingly important in his develop-

ing awareness of the transcendent nature of reality was his insistence on what he sometimes calls "isness," the notion that only in
the verb could one express the kinetic quality of life. In his lecture
about *Eimi,* Cummings' announced topic for the evening was "i &
am & santa claus." And if, as Cummings thought, *The Enormous
Room* was not the "war book" he felt people expected it to be,
it is certainly true that *Eimi* was even less what people expected
it to be: another *Enormous Room.* However, he suggests that there
were in both instances close relationships between what was expected and what was actually presented. *The Enormous Room* used
war, to explore the nature of the individual; *Eimi* explores the
individual again, "a more complex individual in a more enormous
room."

Eimi records Cummings' trip to Russia in 1931. Like *The
Enormous Room,* the book falls logically into three divisions, and,
also like the earlier book, the chronology is based on the geography
of the journey. It began in Paris and occupied thirty-six days, of
which twenty-two were spent in journeying to and staying in
Moscow; eight were spent *en route* to Odessa via Kiev; and six
were spent travelling from Odessa to Istanbul, where he visited
briefly before returning to Paris.

The book is carefully arranged—surely it is more than paradoxi-
cally significant that it opens with the verb SHUT and closes with
the verb OPENS—and, like *The Enormous Room,* it is less a
travelogue than critics and other readers apparently expected.
Cummings kept a rather detailed journal on his trip to Russia, and
it is easy to see that *Eimi* is a deciphering of what the author has
called "on-the-spot-scribbled-hieroglyphics." The notes which
Cummings reworked for *The Enormous Room* were much sketchier;
hence, that book is more an expansion of the notes than a trans-
mutation of them. The effect of the difference in technique is a
powerful one; *Eimi* has a sense of immediacy that the earlier book
lacks. That is its happiest virtue; it is also responsible for its
difficulty.

The reader approaching the book might be well-advised to do so
through the author's "Sketch for a Preface to the Fourth Edition
of *Eimi,*" with which the Grove Press edition of the book opens.
In that sketch Cummings discusses briefly the title, subject, structure, and characters of the book, after which he gives a very brief

day-by-day summary of his activities. This part of the sketch is particularly useful, because Cummings indicated parenthetically the page references for the events he summarizes. There is also a glossary of Russian words, which gives an approximate pronunciation and a meaning for each of the Russian words and phrases used in the book. Though there is no evidence that he ever said so, Cummings' purpose in using the occasional Russian words and phrases seems to have been identical with his stated reason for using French in *The Enormous Room*: to make it clear that a particular character is speaking French (here, Russian), not English. At any rate, there is not enough Russian in the book to cause any problem. Its use does contribute to the overall effect of immediacy which was Cummings' aim. It also serves to remind the reader that the protagonist is a traveller in a strange land and that his one refuge is his journal or diary. The apparent obscurity of the style can be minimized by an understanding that the book makes use of some of the characteristics of the conceptual vocabulary which Cummings employed in his poems. As Friedman has pointed out, the language of the book makes extensive and meaningful use of two prefixes and a suffix: "non-," "un-," and "-less." Systematic use of these affixes enables Cummings to suggest by his very language the negation which he feels to be the dominant characteristic of life in Russia.

Cummings was not, by the way, entirely alone in his reaction to the quality of life in Russia in the 1930's. While many American intellectuals were sufficiently attracted to Communism to become party members, Cummings' rejection of Communism was shared by such people as his friend John Dos Passos, who later had this to say about the conclusion of his stay in Russia in 1928:

> I liked and admired the Russian people. I had enjoyed their enormous and varied country, but when next morning I crossed the Polish border—Poland was not Communist then—it was like being let out of jail. (*The Best Times*, p. 196)

Russia occasionally reminded Cummings, too, of jail, specifically of the enormous room of *La Ferté Macé*. There were happy moments during his journey from SHUT to OPENS, but there is also an overwhelming sense of deliberately structured oppression and negation. Life is a dreary succession of interminable waiting in line for things either no longer available or not worth waiting for in the first place, almost unimaginable tangles of red-tape, and endless dealings with a bureaucracy that is omnipresent, continually tripping one up, catching him off guard, sending him reeling a hundred steps back for every one he takes forward. The passage which most perfectly captures all these aspects of life in Russia, possibly also the best-known single passage, since it was included in Cummings' sixth Harvard lecture, is the description of his visit to Lenin's tomb. It is preceded by an earlier visit to the Metropole to find out when it's open. Nobody there agrees with anyone else on the subject, so Cummings has to go to the tomb itself to find out the hours it is open. He returns the next day and faces the inevitable queue:

facefacefaceface
    hand-
          fin-
              claw
    foot-
       hoof
    (tovarich)
             es to number of numberlessness(un
    -smiling)
with dirt's dirty dirtier with others' dirt with dirt of themselves dirstiest waitstand dirtily never smile shufflebudge dirty pausehalt Smilingless.
              Some from nowhere(faces of nothing)others out of somewhere(somethingshaped hands)these knew ignorance(hugest feet and believing)those were friendless(stopping in their deathskins)all—
numberlessly
—eachotherish
facefacefaceface
facefaceface
faceface
Face
    : all(of whom-which move-do-not-move numberlessly)Toward
the
    Tomb
           Crypt
                Shrine
Grave.
The grave.

Toward the(grave.
All toward the grave)of himself of herself(all toward the grave of
themselves)all toward the grave of Self.
(pp. 240–241)

In terms of symbolic narrative, the author is approaching—
significantly moving down into—the center of the Inferno, where
he will see Satan himself. Cummings identifies himself as an
American correspondent and is quickly moved to the front of the
line. He looks on Lenin briefly and then leaves. The events leave
this impression:

> Certainly it was not made of flesh. And I have seen so many wax-
> works which were actual (some ludicrous more horrible most both)
> so many images whose, very unaliveness could liberate Is, invent
> Being(or what equally disdains life and unlife)—I have seen so very
> many better god or stranger, many mightier deeper puppets; every-
> where and elsewhere and perhaps in America and(of instance)in
> Coney Island . . .
> (p. 243)

It is Communism which Cummings says he rejects in this book;
the reader is occasionally reminded, however, that his rejection is
based on the dehumanizing and brutalizing aspects of Russian
Communism in the 1920's, and that other "-isms" can, and indeed
by definition do also dehumanize and brutalize. In an encounter
with a Russian artist there is this interesting ideological exchange:

> . . .& appear letters, words;skilfully which to the human eye had
> masqueraded as design—as something ornamentally more or less
> emanated by the driver of a troika;but a regular troika;whose steeds
> (unlike Durov's)are not canine . . .& now(whisper)"you read Russ-
> ian?"
> "I can read the Russian letters"I also whisper"but I dough-
> knough what the Russian words mean"
> he gave me a German verb
> ("to drive out?" I guess)
> "da!" upglancing keenly;with much the same(I feel)unmalicious
> mischief which had greeted our heroless from a stage-tovarich-
> sailor's eye at The Last Decisive. "Yes" he purred happily
> "is that capitalism which the driver is Driving Out?" I ask
> "da. Yah:yes!"
> "very neat" I comment,remembering trick-gadgets chez com-

rade flowerbuyer and wondering if comrade Thurston had Russian
blood.

"Here—a-nother. Good. . . . Fight"(it was a smaller box
adorned with battlescene)"more cheap" slyly bozo observes

"no" boldly K states "I like your first box better. The painting is
more Russian"

"why"(sharply)

"the painting of the man driving the horses" sternly I protest "is
more here"(pointing to my bosom)"and I feel that in his heart is
where a Russian lives;and that's why I like the first box better"

"but you do not like the writing" he said as quickly as a mouse
does not move

"O yes"

(startled)"you—are not . . . a cap-italist?"

I hear myself now,laughing now gaily for perhaps the now 1st
time since a town called Paris—"no artist ever is a capitalist!" (pp.
225–226)

Cummings' departure is accompanied by a series of crises involving tickets and visas and his passport. He is clearly relieved
when he is finally out; as he leaves Constantinople, he watches the
sunset—not hell's Red, he notes—and recalls Hell:

USSR a USSR a night- USSR a nightmare USSR home for the pan-
acea Negation haven of all(in life's name)Deathworshippers hopper
of hate's Becausemachine(U for un- & S for self S for science and R
for -reality)how it shrivels:how it dwindles withers;how it wilts
diminishes wanes, how it crumbles evaporates collapses disappears—
the verily consubstantial cauchemar of premeditated NYET (p. 413)

The book had an interesting reception, part of which was due
to the fact that the "leftwing literati," as Norman calls them,
thought—mistakenly—that they had an ally in Cummings. While
he was in Russia, he had—at the request of the Revolutionary
Literature Bureau—done a translation into English of Louis Aragon's Marxist poem, "Le Front Rouge." His translation, "The Red
Front," appeared in Literature of the World Revolution, No. 3, in
1931. Thus Cummings appeared an ally of Marxism. In fact, he
had agreed to do the translation not for ideological reasons at all,
but from friendship and gratitude. Aragon had been a friend of his
in Paris; by the time Cummings planned his trip to Russia, Aragon
had become an ardent Marxist and had acquired a Russian wife, at
whose request Cummings delivered gifts to relatives in Moscow.

It was after all this that he was asked to do the translation. Cummings regarded Aragon's poem as a "hymn of hate"; he gives a very candid opinion of the poem, as well as a brief analysis of it, in *Eimi* (the translation is included in the *Miscellany* collection).

Cummings made his first public pronouncement regarding his stay in Russia in a front-page interview in the Paris edition of the *Chicago Tribune*, June 29, 1931; in that interview he made it clear that he had not liked what he had seen. Thus it became known that Cummings was not a Party ally. It is understandable that the book was not praised by Marxist critics.

Strange attention was paid the book in some quarters. Among the critics who singled the book out for special attention was George Jean Nathan, editor of the *American Spectator*. Nathan, who had once been an associate of H. L. Mencken on the *American Mercury*, had previously offered a rather disagreeable comment on Cummings' play *Him*. When he became editor of the *American Spectator*, he instituted a new department called "The Worst Book of the Month." In the April, 1933, issue, *Eimi* was the featured book in that department. That is particularly interesting in view of the fact that there were neither bound copies nor galleys of the book available at the time the April *Spectator* went to press. No one has ever explained how Nathan managed to read the book before selecting it for his new department. Since the first review, *Eimi* has always had a poorer press than it deserves. Perhaps it, too, is due for a revival. It has, in recent years, been a little better known for its mention in Cummings' nonlectures.

These lectures themselves, delivered at Harvard in 1952–1953, were immensely popular and influential, and they were later published in two forms: a printed text of the lectures, together with the readings with which Cummings concluded each lecture, and a set of recordings made during the lectures. Like all Cummings' full-length prose works, the collection of lectures is something which defies classification. The title warns the reader not to expect any usual sort of thing. Cummings called his talks at Harvard "nonlectures" and the book is a collection of "nonlectures." It is also a brief anthology of selected key passages from his own writings, as well as a small, highly personal collection of some of the best poems of western literature.

Of greatest interest, though, is what Cummings has to say

about himself and his development as an artist. He is in some important ways a unique figure among American artists of the twentieth century, and it is good to have light cast on his particular stance as an individual. Friedman has spoken of him as a paradoxer, and his own life is full of the kinds of contradiction and ambivalence that call to mind again the tradition of American writers from which Cummings partly sprang. Cummings greatly valued his privacy, so it is in some ways almost astonishing that he put into the lectures the very personal material which forms the heart of them. In the first two of them he describes his father and mother, his childhood home, his early friends and first books. One early reviewer, Robert Graves, found all this a bit "corny" and longed for more of the author's "Old Carnality," but the majority of readers seem to be charmed, rather than otherwise. It is not unheard of for an individual to have a happy childhood, and Cummings does seem to have had one. Lecture Three has to do with his "selfdiscovery": in it, he traces his adolescent development. For his discovery of self he thanks Harvard and all that life there involved, including independence. After Harvard, he thanks the "phenomenon and miracle" known as New York City, and then Paris, whose freedom, he said, surpassed that he had found in New York as much as that he had found in New York surpassed that of Harvard:

> Thus thru an alma mater whose scholastic bounty appeared the smallest of her blessings—and by way of the even more magnificent institutions of learning, New York and Paris—our ignoramus reaches his supreme indebtedness. Last but most, I thank for my self-finding certain beautiful givers of illimitable gladness
>> whose any mystery makes every man's
>> flesh put space on;and his mind take off time
>> (pp. 53–54)

Beginning with Lecture Four, Cummings presents his stance as a writer; he does that through the three remaining lectures, the topics of which are respectively "i & you & is," "i & now & him," and "i & am & santa claus." In each Cummings puts himself as a writer on display, primarily by devoting the greater part of each lecture to quotations from his works, arranged chronologically in lectures four and five. In the final lecture he reads from *Eimi* and *Santa Claus* and then concludes by answering a question raised in

131

Lecture One, after which he leaves his audience in the company of
two poets he admires:

> So ends the last lesson of a nondivisible ignoramus: a double
> lesson—outwardly and inwardly affirming that,whereas a world
> rises to fall, a spirit descends to ascend. Now our ignoramus faces
> the nonanswerable question "who, as a writer, am I?" with which
> his nonlecturing career began; and finds himself deluged by multi-
> tudinous answers. What would these multitudinous answers say if
> they could speak as a single answer? Possibly or impossibly this—
>
> I am someone who proudly and humbly affirms that love is the
> mystery-of-mysteries, and that nothing measurable matters "a very
> good God damn:" that "an artist, a man, a failure" is no mere
> whenfully accreting mechanism, but a givingly eternal complexity—
> neither some soulless and heartless utrapredatory infra-animal nor
> any un-understandingly knowing and believing and thinking auto-
> mation, but a naturally and miraculously whole human being—a
> feelingly illimitable individual; whose only happiness is to transcend
> himself, whose every agony is to grow.
>
> Ecstasy and anguish, being and becoming; the immortality of the
> creative imagination and the indomitability of the human spirit—
> these are the subjects of my final poetry reading: which (I devoutly
> hope) may not wrong a most marvellous ode by Keats, and the
> magnificent closing stanzas of Shelley's Prometheus Unbound. (pp.
> 110–111)

Cummings' final prose publication was the joint venture with
his wife, a collection of fifty photographs by Marion Morehouse
and captions by Cummings. The photographs themselves are a fine
and rich collection, important and interesting in their own right.
The captions make them even more interesting; they are also of in-
trinsic interest. They are brief, most of them; they range in length
from a single word to full-page essays. The latter occur exclusively
in the final section of the book, "People," always Cummings' main
interest. These essays are all tributes—some to famous people, like
Marianne Moore, some to people not so famous—to individuals
lovingly portrayed. The best of the captions remind one of
the best of Cummings' poems; they employ a technique summarized in one of the short captions: "note the nail." Cummings
had spent a lifetime noting nails and driving them home. *Adventures in Value* was published in the Fall of 1962, shortly after
Cummings' death in September of that year.

5
The Drama

Curiously, one is more apt to chance upon a performance of some of Cummings' poems set to music than a performance of any of the three plays, *Him, Anthropos,* and *Santa Claus.* The ballet *Tom* has apparently never been produced. All are available to the reader, however, in the collection *E. E. Cummings: Three Plays and a Ballet* (1967), edited by George J. Firmage. Additionally, one can hear readings from *Him* and *Santa Claus* in E. E. Cummings' recordings of *i:six nonlectures* and other records. The three plays may be due for a revival of interest. Thanks to television, there is probably a potential audience for Cummings' plays for the first time in several decades. This is because television has revived the burlesque tradition, most successfully in such series as America's "Laugh-In" and Britain's "Up Pompeii." It is a tradition with which Cummings was very familiar, as we know. We have seen that many of his poems refer directly to burlesque as he knew it on the American stage in the 1920's and that others are written in what can be called the burlesque style. Similarly, the plays both allude to and participate in the style of burlesque, a style which makes use of such devices as exaggeration, illusion, above all movement.

In a reversal of the usual arrangement, *Him* was published before it was ever produced. Excerpts—all or part of Act I, Scene II, Act II, Scene VI, and Act III, Scenes I, V, VI, and VII of the finished play—appeared in *The Dial* for August, 1927; the whole work appeared in book form in November of that year. Unorthodox though it was—it was frankly experimental in nature, and contained twenty-one scenes and a hundred and five characters—it was taken seriously by critics, all of whom assumed, however, that it was fated to remain a closet drama. It was performed at the Provincetown Theatre, though, with all roles played by a cast of thirty people. It ran for twenty-seven performances, beginning April 10, 1928; it closed when it did because it was such an expensive production.

While it ran, the play attracted large audiences. The critics, almost to a man, denounced it. Even the kindlier of the uptown critics could manage nothing better than the suggestion that Cummings appeared to view life as a combination of the familiar domestic situation of a man with a dumb wife and a sophomoric burlesque show. One of the most severe of the critics, George Jean Nathan, wrote of the play that for sheer guff, it had never been surpassed within his memory. He spoke of it as incoherent, illiterate, and idiotic. He concluded his attack by turning his attention to Cummings the man, whom he identified as "a sub-Gertrude Stein in pants, a ridiculous adolescent in revolt against literary tradition with a hair pin" (Norman, p. 226).

This outburst was typical in that it was directed more at the playwright than the play; it seems curious today that such antipathy toward a man could result in such a display of emotion over an avowedly *avant-garde* production. Indeed, it has been noted that what was most surprising about the unfavorable criticism was that its intemperate wrath seemed completely out of proportion to the stimulus. Nathan and others may have been initially offended by the advice offered on the program for *Him*:

> Relax and give this PLAY a chance to strut its stuff—relax, don't worry because it's not like something else—relax, stop wondering what it's all "about"—like many strange and familiar things, Life included, this PLAY isn't "about," it simply is. Don't try to despise it, let it try to despise you. Don't try to enjoy it, let it try to enjoy you. DON'T TRY TO UNDERSTAND IT, LET IT TRY TO UNDERSTAND YOU. (Norman, p. 223)

The advice indicates that Cummings expected the play to be controversial. It also suggests a certain dominant theme of the play, a view of man that turns him inside out, putting him on display when he least expects it. Anyone who has ever stood before the monkey cage at the zoo and watched the monkeys watch the people will recognize that theme as an important part of the reality of experience in *Him*. That kind of depiction of reality was unique in American drama at the time *Him* appeared. In technique, it represented Cummings' efforts to use some of the devices of expressionism which were still new in European theater, such devices as mirrors, rotating sets, indirect presentation of conflict and resolution, and picture-frame scenes. It might even be considered one of the first examples of what is now called the theater of the absurd. Certainly, it was influenced by such playwrights as the German Expressionists.

In addition to the "advice" Cummings had given his spectator, he had also provided on the program an "Imaginary Dialogue Between the Author and a Public as Imagined by E. E. Cummings" (it had originally appeared on the dust jacket), a dialogue which suggests other themes important in the play. When the Public says airily that "nonsense isn't everything in life," the Author replies

> And so far as you're concerned "life" is a verb of two voices— active, to do, and passive, to dream. Others believe doing to be only a kind of dreaming. Still others have discovered (in a mirror surrounded by mirrors), something harder than silence but softer than falling; the third voice of "life," which believes itself and which cannot mean because it is: (Norman, p. 210)

Another item of interest that serves as a useful introduction to *Him* is a description of the work that appeared on the inside back flap of the dust jacket. Written by Isidor Schneider of the advertising department of Boni & Liveright, the book's publisher, it offered what Cummings considered an excellent "Statement to a Certain Public by a Certain Publisher":

> There is good reason for Mr Cummings' crypticism in his description of *Him*. We do not remember any book that more baffles an attempt to describe it.
>
> You may think you know what to expect in a play by Cummings —and you will find out that you don't know the half of it. Such lucid madness, such adventurous gayety, such graceful irreverence, such abounding novelties—squads of characters firing broadsides of wit—interpolations of American folklore, extravagances that astound the imagination. It is a play that satisfies the five senses, and every

corner of the intelligence—a play full of revels for the grown-up mind. (Norman, p. 210)

The key word, as is frequently true with Cummings, is *play*. Play can be serious, as well as frivolous, however, and that in *Him* is very serious, though never somber. The plot involves the discovery on the part of what Cummings calls a "would-be artist" that his difficulty in writing (and he is writing a play) springs from an inability to love. That inability to love springs in turn from a lack of a sense of identity. Today he might announce that he is in the throes of an identity crisis, victim perhaps of a generation gap. There is no formal resolution in the play; as it ends, the would-be artist is beginning to realize the nature of his problem. The tentative and ambiguous ending to the play is another reason to call the play expressionistic.

So puzzled were the critics that there was no consensus on the meaning. So varied were the reactions, and so different were the opinions of the uptown critics from those of some serious writers that the Provincetown ultimately published a thin brochure contrasting these views. Gilbert Seldes wrote the Introduction to "*Him* and the Critics: A Collection of Opinions on E. E. Cummings' Play at the Provincetown Playhouse," which was dedicated to John Anderson, one of the critics who praised the play. Anderson thought its technique original and said that it was a "shrewd and believable scheme" for reducing to dramatic form the "stream of consciousness" more often dealt with in the novel.

Friedman's book *The Growth of a Writer* gives a rather detailed scene-by-scene analysis of the action of the play. In it, he suggests that it is possible to understand that the "play within the play" in Act II is written by Him, who tells Me that the play is written by The Other Man (i.e. the Man in the Mirror, i.e. the husband-self that the artist in Him is struggling not to be) in order that he may attempt to integrate in her eyes, as well as his own, his two selves. Him's two selves are not integrated in the play; neither are Me's two selves—the mistress and the wife remain separate. That is responsible for the real terror in Him's reaction to the discovery that Me has borne a child. Even before Him has "found himself" in one reality, that reality has been transformed: Baby makes three.

The main objection to Cummings' play *Him* was that it was formless; that apparent formlessness was deliberate and may, of course, be explained on the grounds that he was trying to depict a life-picture which was itself formless. In view of the present state of the American stage, it seems doubly unfortunate that *Him*'s reception was not kinder. If Cummings' attempts to depict life by using the techniques of the European experimental theater along with those of the American burlesque stage and the circus had not met with such an unkind reception, Cummings and other American playwrights might have gone far toward nurturing a productive tradition of the non-realistic theater.

As it was, Cummings' further career as a playwright was limited to the slight works *Anthropos* and *Tom*, and the short play *Santa Claus*. *Anthropos: or the Future of Art*, to give it its full title, was first published in a collection entitled *Whither, Whither, or After Sex What? A Symposium to End Symposiums* (1930). A small limited edition of the play was published in 1944. It is really more a skit than a play; the whole of the action might have occupied no more than three scenes of *Him*.

There are no formal divisions within the work, which opens on part of the "dim interior of a hemispherical cave" and closes in utter darkness. The characters include "three uncouth infrahuman creatures" in dirty skins, a primitive artist, and a mob. The three creatures, called only by the initials *G*, *O*, and *D*, are busy inventing slogans. As they talk, and as the artist continues work on a line drawing on the cave wall, sounds of modern technology—planes and other machines—grow in intensity. Comments such as "You must interest their imagination, G" and "They're just children after all, you know" make it clear that the creatures are seeking a slogan to pacify the masses. The three announce simultaneously "I GOT IT" and give the word "Ev.O.Lution" followed by a cheer. They congratulate one another, then summon—from the direction of the audience—a mob of "hide-smothered infrahuman dwarfs," angry until they hear the magic word. At this point the artist leaves his unfinished work, announcing that he has "got to have another look" at the mammoth outside. The creatures remind him that civilization, emancipation, and progress—"the Ford's truth! So help me Lenin!"—have eliminated monsters. Then the artist jerks aside a curtain and reveals in all its questionable glory, a steamshovel. The artist leaves, and the play concludes in the now familiar manner of the theater of the absurd; conversation is resumed, and one creature says, "Well, as I was saying. . . ."

It has been suggested that the play is important in that it anticipated *Santa Claus*. Friedman has suggested that in it the politicians equal Death, the artist equals Santa Claus, and the mob is always and ever the mob, synonymous with the "mostpeople" of Cummings' poetry. Certainly the themes are familiar enough to Cummings' readers. The nature of man being what it is, the twentieth century is no less barbaric than prehistoric times; "mostpeople" are such creatures of habit that they accept, not only unquestioningly, but unseeingly, the notions and actualities of their culture. Thus, they are truly incapable of understanding that a steamshovel —much touted symbol of civilization, emancipation, and progress —*is* a mammoth, i.e. a monster. The ironic allusions to Ford predate Huxley's caricature of Ford practices in *Brave New World* by two years; in that book, readers will recall, men and women prayed to "the Great Ford" and made the "sign of the T" on their chests. The other important allusion, that to Lenin, is suggestive of the dominant theme of *Eimi*. Most important, however, is the attitude of the artist. In this work Cummings has again dealt with the question of the relationship of the artist to his society. Friedman has pointed out the irony of the fact that the artist's model is itself a mechanical product of civilization—but that the artist's concern with the machine is to recreate it, not use it. This recalls the very important statement of Cummings that the artist's chief concern is with *making*, that he is a man to whom things *made* matter very little.

Tom, the ballet based on the novel by Harriet Beecher Stowe, is a curious work. Written specifically to be produced as a ballet in which the narrative would be translated into choreography, it must be examined here as a piece of literature. In structure it is simple. The "synopsis" describes in brief each of the four episodes, each of which is then presented in terms of dance description, complete with staging details—lighting, etc.

Interestingly, the work is written in such a style that it can stand on its own as a work of dramatic narrative; in it Cummings demonstrates his ability to render poetic whatever material he is

working with. It is a real delight to discover that the artistry of
Cummings is such that he could take the plot of a propaganda
novel written by an abolitionist, transform its theme from one
advocating a doctrinaire solution to the question of slavery to one
showing love triumphant over hate, and present the result as a set
of choreographic directions become poetry.

Cummings' last play made its initial appearance as *Santa Claus
(A Morality)* in the Spring, 1946, issue of *The Harvard Wake*, a
special Cummings number, appearing in book form later that same
year. It is for two reasons an appropriate finale to his "career" as
a playwright: it is the most mature of all the dramatic writings,
and thus pays tribute to Cummings' continued growth as an artist,
and it embodies some of the same kinds of lyrical affirmation as
some of the best poems.

Santa Claus is both more realistic and less personal than *Him*,
its most important predecessor. It is simpler in design, if more
allegorical in structure. The action, performed by four principals,
other voices, and a mob, is divided into five scenes. Of the
principals, two—Santa Claus and Death—are dominant. The
whole of Scene One is a dialogue between them in which Santa
Claus initially laments the fact that he wants to give, but can find
no takers; Death's problem—"also one of distribution"—is that
he has so much to take, but can find no givers. Death offers his
help to Santa Claus, who accepts it, as a result of which he is
immediately instructed in what turn out to be the principles of
survival in a capitalistic society. Santa Claus is offering "understanding"; in the world he inhabits, "a world so blurred/ that its
inhabitants are one another," only knowledge commands a price.
As Death puts it, understanding is the only gift, and therein lies
the predicament:

> We are not living in an age of gifts:
> this is an age of salesmanship, my friend,
> and you are heavy with the only thing
> which simply can't be sold. (p. 128)

In this world, anybody can sell knowledge, because everybody
wants knowledge. Santa Claus agrees to become a knowledge-
salesman, that is, a scientist. When he does so, Death removes the
mask from Santa Claus's face, revealing that of a young man, and
exchanges it for his own, underneath which is a fleshless human

skull. Once they have exchanged masks, Death gives his final instructions:

> . . .—in this "Science" game, this "Knowledge" racket,
> infinity's your limit; but remember:
> the less something exists, the more people want it. (p. 129)

As Santa Claus seems unable to think of anything which doesn't exist, Death suggests he sell "wheelmines," and Santa agrees to do so.

Scene Two opens with Santa Claus, masked as Death, haranguing a mob. He demonstrates his abilities as a huckster by selling a great deal of "preferred stock in a giltedged wheelmine," after which he delivers a speech in which he tells the Mob that Science will free them from their "obscene humanity" by the process of capitalism:

> —While men were merely men, and nothing more,
> what was equality? A word. A dream.
> Men never could be equal. Why? Because
> equality's the attribute of supermen
> like you, and you, and you. And therefore
> (superladies and supergentlemen)
> when the impartial ear of Science hears
> your superhuman voices crying "gimme,"
> Science responds in Its omnipotence
> "let there be enough wheelmine stock for all." (p. 132)

Joyfully, the mob accept bread and circuses—"Adda baby! Long live Science! Hooray for wheelmines!"—and do not notice that they have been substituted for the light of understanding.

In Scene Three Death appears, masked as Santa Claus. Hearing angry voices offstage, he exults: "I've got him now!" Santa Claus, masked at Death, runs onstage, fleeing an irate mob. Questioned by Death, he explains that there's been an accident in the wheelmine. Reminded that the wheelmine does not exist, Santa Claus asks poignantly:

> O, then tell me:
> how can it maim, how can it mutilate;
> how can it turn mere people into monsters:
> answer me—how!
> (p. 133)

To the obvious question, Death gives a logical answer:

My friend, you've forgotten something:
namely, that people, like wheelmines, don't exist
—two negatives, you know, make an affirmative. (p. 133)

The audience is aware, of course, that while two negatives make a positive where logic (science, knowledge) is concerned, they do no such thing in other realms. The audience is also aware of what Santa Claus learns only at this point, that he is indeed dealing with Death, who leaves just as the furious Mob enter, followed by a little girl. Santa Claus escapes the fury of the mob by convincing them he doesn't exist; this he does by calling on the little girl, who promptly identifies "Mr Science" as Santa Claus.

Scene Four opens on Santa Claus, still masked as Death, musing "That was a beautiful child . . . If only I were sure—"; he breaks off to greet Death, also still masked. It is Death's turn to ask a favor; he wants to impress a woman who "favors plump men," so he arranges to exchange his skeleton for Santa's fat. They exchange clothes, at which point they completely resemble each other. Upon Death's exit, the child enters, revealing by her conversation that she is looking for someone, a beautiful and sad someone, who is sad because she and the child have lost each other—"and somebody else." At the very end of the scene, the child tells Santa that *he* is the somebody else.

Scene Five, very brief, opens with a woman weeping:

Knowledge has taken love out of the world
and all the world is empty empty empty:
men are not men any more in all the world
for a man who cannot love is not a man,
and only a woman in love can be a woman;
and, from their love alone, joy is born—joy! (p. 138)

She calls out for death to release her from her misery; at that point Santa Claus, disguised as Death, enters and announces that he will take her "now and forever." In a final sequence of events reminiscent of the closing scene in *Tom*, Santa Claus comforts the woman, and the mob, who have been heard offstage, carry in a pole from which is suspended the corpse of Death, still disguised as Santa Claus. The child returns; Santa Claus claims her as his own, and then unmasks.

The message is clearly allegorical, Death and an unworld (mob, mostpeople) opposing three individuals separated from each other. Death attempts to keep them separated, but is foiled, initially by the child, finally by his own "cleverness" in disguising himself as Santa Claus in order to try to fool the woman, who is certainly that "swell Jane" who "prefers plump fellows." Death is disposed of by the mob, and the three individuals are re-united as a loving triumvirate, which was still an impossible situation in *Him*.

The message is certainly social, as well; Cummings himself suggested (in his sixth "nonlecture") that in *Santa Claus* he was examining the "phenomenon" of

> a spiritually impotent pseudocommunity enslaved by perpetual obscenities of mental concupiscence; an omnivorous social hypocrisy vomiting vitalities of idealism while grovelling before the materialization of its own deathwish: a soi-disant free society, dedicated to immeasurable generosities of love; but dominated by a mere and colossal lust for knowing, which threatens not simply to erase all past and present and future human existence but to annihilate (in the name of liberty) Life herself.
> (*i:six nonlectures*, p. 103)

And the message is couched in that very traditional form, blank verse, which has long and generally been accepted as that best adapted to dramatic verse in English. Cummings had travelled a long way from *Him*, both in dramatic structure and style. Friedman has summarized the journey as being essentially one which began as a fairly literal presentation of the problem of the human trinity—father, mother, child—and concluded as a highly allegorical presentation of a suggested solution, that in which the child is the redeemer, the agent who through love re-unites the trinity. That the accompanying shift in style is one which moves from the very lyrical prose of *Him* to the traditional blank verse of Santa Claus may say more about the nature of theater and its relationship with the English language than it does about Cummings himself.

6

An Appraisal

Cummings' literary works, particularly his poetry, have had a somewhat curious critical history. The reasons for this are varied; some are quite accidental, others are rather basic to intent and method. For his recent collection, *E. E. CUMMINGS: A COLLECTION OF CRITICAL ESSAYS* (1972), Norman Friedman wrote an introductory essay which explores the curious nature of that history and undertakes to examine the causes of it. As Friedman points out in the essay, in relation to the critical and academic establishments, there has always been a slight flavor of illegitimacy where Cummings is concerned. He suggests that the main reason for Cummings' curious critical reception through the decades is that he was never writing the kind of poetry that was fashionable. He early aroused hostility on the part of antimodernists like Max Eastman and Stanton A. Coblenz and later John Sparrow and Ivor Winters. These were the men who were attacking Pound and Eliot as well. By the 1930's, though, New Critics such as R. P. Blackmur were beginning to be made somewhat uneasy by Cummings' romanticism and what appeared to them to be over-simplified answers to the problems of the day.

It was not until the 1940's that some critics—Lloyd Frankenberg was an early one—realized that there was a great deal more to Cummings than had met the eyes of previous beholders. Even then there were problems, for in the classrooms of colleges and universities across the United States, the methods of the New Criticism had become firmly entrenched. The New Criticism's particular method of close analysis, with its emphasis on searching out particular kinds of ambiguity, did not suit Cummings' poems very well. Its concern with image and symbol, to the relative exclusion of genre or form, obviously makes it somewhat un-suited for dealing with poetry which makes only limited use of symbol and imagery and which does not rely on allusion as an important way of communicating. As we have seen, his poems yield riches to the careful reader, but they must be searched out on their own terms.

When a particular critical theory does not suit a particular writer—i.e. does not examine his works to best advantage—it does not follow that there is anything wrong either with the theory or with the writer. There may, however, be something very wrong with the application of the theory. With Cummings, of course, as with any other writer, the first critical principle is to deal with what the writer has actually done, not what he might have done if he had been someone else. It is to the credit of critics like Friedman that more recent studies have finally explored the reality of Cummings' achievement in language. It should, in the future, be possible for Cummings' admirers to feel less called upon to *defend* him. They will then be able to explore more fully his vision of this universe and the techniques through which he sought to share his vision. Some of the specific techniques used by Cummings to share his vision of the universe have been discussed. What has not been discussed is the broad implication of his use of specific poetic techniques. While his techniques of typography, capitalization, punctuation, etc., are all very interesting in and of themselves, they are even more interesting when considered together as a pattern of linguistic signalling. Their major significance seems to be as what we might call code-labels; they signal a level of usage and therefore have a function other than that of carrying a message—though they also do that, of course, and on several levels. Of great significance where Cummings' writings are concerned is the fact that he makes greater use of intimate and casual styles than other poets writing at the same time (I use these terms as they are defined by Martin Joos in his linguistic excursion into the five styles of English usage, *The Five Clocks*), so much so that he may be said to have deliberately used the characteristic features of intimate and casual styles, where other poets might have used casual and consultative styles. He did so, I think, because he felt that conventional language usage—consultative style for consultation, casual style for casual discourse, etc.—was bankrupt. He made an attempt to break down certain barriers between himself and his reader. He did this by treating his reader with a greater degree of intimacy than his reader was always prepared for. Many of his poems have the external features of highly intimate letters. Some readers have been put off by some of the poems, I think, because they have felt unable to respond to such intimacy. These people are in the position of having opened letters that appear not to be directed to them. They are, I think, somewhat embarrassed and perhaps a little resentful. Theirs is an unfortunate, if natural reaction.

In addition to using the intimate style so often, Cummings also deviated from general usage by mixing styles, using more than two in alternation, occasionally jumping steps. In ordinary discourse, a speaker—or writer—confines himself to two neighboring styles alternately, it being considered anti-social for a speaker to shift two or more steps in a single jump, for instance from casual to formal. Cummings' disregard for this convention is, I think, partly responsible for the critical reception of some of his early poetry, where he most blatantly mixed styles. The early poems in which style-mixing is most obvious are those in which there is a mixture of archaisms and colloquialisms. Here is one example:

> being
> twelve
> who hast merely
> gonorrhea
>
>   Oldeyed
> child, to
> ambitious weeness
> of boots
>
> tiny
> add
> death
> what
>
> shall?
> (I, 105)

✳ Cummings' deviation from convention is certainly not the result of carelessness or ignorance. It amounts to a deliberate and highly informed departure from the rules of conventional discourse. The rules are those of his early life, and they are important as much when they are being challenged as when they are being followed blindly. We must not forget that Cummings was as thoroughly a product of his milieu as any American poet, and even his radical poetry is a constant reminder that he was formed by the area bounded by Boston's State House, Harvard University, the Charles River, the Field of Lexington, and Concord's bridge. It is not possible to deviate from rules which are not thoroughly established; there is, therefore, a certain amount of implied respect for the conventions of his early environment in all of Cummings' writings.

I have used the word "radical" in connection with Cummings' poetry; he was radical in his metaphysics and in his anti-societal stance, certainly. He was linguistically radical in the sense that his wit is concerned with the roots of syntax and grammar. He shows throughout his poetry great consciousness of the close relationship between life and grammar. That relationship is explored most fully in a love poem:

> since feeling is first
> who pays any attention
> to the syntax of things
> will never wholly kiss you,
>
> wholly to be a fool
> while Spring is in the world
>
> my blood approves,
> and kisses are a better fate
> than wisdom
> lady i swear by all flowers. Don't cry
> —the best gesture of my brain is less than
> your eyelids' flutter which says
>
> we are for each other: then
> laugh, leaning back in my arms
> for life's not a paragraph

And death i think is no parenthesis
(I, 290)

His very words here belie any interpretation of the poem which
depends on an anti-intellectual bias on Cummings' part. He ex-
presses his reverence for the non-logical in terms based on grammatical categories. That he can do so indicates a reverence for
form. Grammatical categories are the elements with which we
create order (i.e. language) out of chaos (i.e. sounds). It is clear
that Cummings scorns neither logic nor thought. He thinks them
less important, in the final analysis, than feeling and emotion,
particularly love—and most especially so when "Spring is in the
world"—but he clearly has a place for them in his scheme of
things.

There is, thus, no reason to think of Cummings as a simple-
minded idealist. Nor is he a romantic in the nineteenth-century
sense of that term. He has been called a "neo-romantic" and perhaps he is. Friedman has called him a Paradoxer. Clearly of the
twentieth-century, Cummings does not fit neatly into twentieth-
century categories. If he is a "neo-romantic," it is important
to distinguish between his quest and those of such people
as Novalis, looking for his little blue flower, and Dostoevsky's
Underground Man, determined that two plus two shall be five,
out of spite. Cummings certainly reveals himself to be a transcendentalist, but he is as far from being a romantic, in any
"pure" sense of that word, as his volume title *is 5* is from that
illogical statement that two plus two is five.

Cummings' major accomplishments were two: first of all, he
revived the lyric as a viable poetic form and transformed it greatly,
enlarging its horizons and multiplying its poetic possibilities;
second, he created a poetic language by means of which he forced
his reader to consider action, motivation, and character from view-
points new to him. At his best, he forced the reader into the kind
of re-reading that results in the finest kind of education available
to most of us, that in which we continue to educate ourselves.

I do not think that poets can be ranked or graded. I would not
know where to put Cummings on a numerical scale, nor would I
know whether he should be judged an $A+$ or $B-$ poet. He clearly
has a place among the leading poets writing in English in the

twentieth century. He was in some interesting ways a poet ahead of his time, particularly with respect to his achievement in bending language to his will. In that respect, he was different from some other important poets of the century. While others are now *behind* us, he is, I think, often still *ahead* of us. For that reason, it is still too early to define his place in twentieth-century literature, though we can say that in some respects it will be found to be to one side of the poets who constitute the various "main-streams" of twentieth-century English and American poetry. Twin streams merge in Cummings, those of traditionalism and innovation, and they do so in ways that they do not in other poets of the century. Ideologically, Cummings was an American transcendentalist; he sought to express his vision of the transcendent universe by stretching the shape of the lyric poem. His description of himself as "an author of pictures, less a draughtsman of words" re-enforces our own conviction that as a poet he was the most traditional of innovators and the most innovative of traditionalists.

Bibliographical Note

Below are given full bibliographical descriptions of all books to which page references are made parenthetically in the text. Except as noted in the text, all poems are given in their final published form.

Primary Sources

Adventures in Value. New York: Harcourt, Brace & World, Inc., 1962. Fifty photographs by Marion Morehouse with text by E. E. Cummings.

Complete Poems. 2 vols. London: MacGibbon & Kee, 1968. (The pagination is identical in the one-volume *Complete Poems* published by Harcourt Brace Jovanovich, 1972.)

E. E. Cummings: A Miscellany Revised. Ed. George J. Firmage. New York: October House, Inc., 1965. Originally published 1958.

Eight Harvard Poets. New York: Laurence J. Gomme, 1917.

Eimi. New York: Grove Press, Inc., 1958. (Evergreen Book E–113 is the equivalent paperback edition.) Originally published 1933.

i:six nonlectures. Cambridge, Massachusetts: Harvard University Press, 1953. (The paperback edition issued by Atheneum in 1967 has the same pagination.)

Selected Letters. Ed. F. W. Dupee and George Stade. New York: Harcourt, Brace & World, Inc., 1969.

The Enormous Room. New York: Random House Modern Library edition, 1934. Originally published 1922.

Three Plays and a Ballet. Ed. George J. Firmage. New York: October House, Inc., 1967.

Secondary Sources

Aldridge, John W. *After the Lost Generation: A Critical Study of the Writers of Two Wars.* New York: The Noonday Press, 1951. (First Noonday Paperbound Edition, 1958.)

Attaway, Kenneth R. *E. E. Cummings' Aloofness: An Underlying Theme in the Poetry*. Atlanta: Georgia State College, 1969.

Baum, S. V., ed. *EΣTI: eec: E. E. Cummings and the Critics*. East Lansing, Michigan: Michigan State University Press, 1962.

Damon, S. Foster. *Amy Lowell: A Chronicle: With Extracts From Her Correspondence*. Boston and New York: The Houghton Mifflin Company, 1935.

Dos Passos, John. *An Informal Memoir: The Best Times*. New York, The New American Library, 1966.

Frankenberg, Lloyd. *Pleasure Dome: on reading modern poetry* Garden City, New York: Doubleday & Company, Inc., 1949. Reissued 1961.

Friedman, Norman. *e. e. cummings: The Art of His Poetry*. Baltimore: The Johns Hopkins Press, 1960. (The Johns Hopkins Paperback edition, 1967, has the same pagination.)

—— *e. e. cummings: The Growth of a Writer*. Carbondale, Illinois: Southern Illinois University Press, 1964.

Joost, Nicholas. *Scofield Thayer and The Dial: An illustrated History*. Carbondale and Edwardsville, Illinois: Southern Illinois University Press, 1964.

Norman, Charles. *E. E. Cummings: The Magic-Maker*. Indianapolis and New York: The Bobbs-Merrill Company, Inc., 1972. (Earlier editions appeared in 1958 and 1964.)

Wasserstrom, William. *The Time of the Dial*. Syracuse, New York: Syracuse University Press, 1963.

Other secondary works of interest are as follows:

Firmage, George J. *E. E. Cummings: A Bibliography*. Middleton, Connecticut: Wesleyan University Press, 1960.

Friedman, Norman, *E. E. Cummings: A Collection of Critical Essays*. Englewood Cliffs, N. J.: Prentice-Hall, Inc., 1972. (Spectrum Book S-TC-98 in the series Twentieth Century Views.)

Marks, Barry A. *E. E. Cummings*. New York: Twayne Publishers, Inc., 1964. (Twayne's United States Authors Series No. 46.)

Norman, Charles. *Poets & People*. Indianapolis and New York: The Bobbs-Merrill Company, Inc., 1972.

Triem, Eve. *E. E. Cummings*. Minneapolis: University of Minnesota Press, 1969. (No. 87 of the Pamphlets on American Writers.)

Wegner, Robert E. *The Poetry and Prose of E. E. Cummings*. New York: Harcourt, Brace & World, Inc., 1965.

Additional studies have been announced by Richard Kennedy of Temple University and Patricia Tal-Mason Cline of Miami-Dade Junior

BIOGRAPHICAL NOTE

College. The first volume of Professor Kennedy's critical biography, *E. E. Cummings, The Years of Innocence*, will be ready late in 1973; a second volume will appear later. Professor Cline's book will deal with Cummings' spiritual struggle with himself.

Recorded Readings
E. E. Cummings Reads His Poetry. Caedmon Publishers, TC 1017 (12" 33⅓ rpm), 1953.
six nonlectures. 6 Albums. Caedmon Records, Inc., TC 1186, TC 1187, TC 1188, TC 1189, TC 1190, TC 1191 (12" 33⅓ rpm), 1965.

Index of First Lines

Subject Index